생활 속의 참선수행 Practice In Daily Life ⑬

Faith in Action
Learning To Rely Upon Our Root

믿는 만큼 行한 만큼

믿는 만큼 行한 만큼
대행큰스님 법문
생활 속의 참선수행 ⑬ / 한영합본

발행일	2017년 4월 초판1쇄
영문번역	한마음국제문화원
표지디자인	박수연
편집	한마음국제문화원
발행	한마음출판사
출판등록	384-2000-000010
전화	031-470-3175
팩스	031-470-3209
이메일	onemind@hanmaum.org

© 2017(재)한마음선원
본 출판물은 저작권법에 의하여 보호를 받는 저작물이므로
무단 복제와 무단 전재를 할 수 없습니다.

Faith in Action: Learning To Rely Upon Our Root
Practice in Daily Life ⑬ / Bilingual, Korean · English
Dharma Talks by Seon Master Daehaeng

First Edition, First Printing: April 2017
English Translation by
Hanmaum International Culture Institute
Edited by Hanmaum International Culture Institute
Cover Design by Su Yeon Park
Published by Hanmaum Publications
www.hanmaumbooks.org

© 2017 Hanmaum Seonwon Foundation
All rights reserved, including the right to reproduce
this work in any form.

Printed in the Republic of Korea

ISBN 978-89-91857-43-8 (04220) / 978-89-951830-0-7 (set)

국립중앙도서관 출판예정도서목록(CIP)

```
믿는 만큼 行한 만큼 = Faith in Action ; 한영합본 / 대행
큰스님 법문 ; 한마음국제문화원 영문번역. -- [안양] :
한마음출판사, 2017
   p. ;  cm. -- (생활속의 참선수행 =Practice in Daily
Life ; 13)

한영대역본임
ISBN 978-89-91857-43-8 04220 : ₩6000
ISBN 978-89-951830-0-7 (세트) 04220

법문(불경)[法文]

224.2-KDC6
294.34-DDC23                         CIP2017009552
```

이 도서의 국립중앙도서관 출판예정도서목록(CIP)은 서지정보유통지원시스템 홈페이지(http://seoji.nl.go.kr)와 국가자료공동목록시스템(http://www.nl.go.kr/kolisnet)에서 이용하실 수 있습니다.(CIP제어번호: CIP2017009552)

A CIP catalogue record of the National Library of Korea for this book is available at the homepage of CIP(http://seoji.nl.go.kr) and Korean Library Information System Network(http://www.nl.go.kr/kolisnet). (CIP2017009552)

Faith in Action
Learning To Rely Upon Our Root

Seon Master Daehaeng

믿는 만큼 行한 만큼

대행큰스님 법문

차 례

10 머리글

12 대행큰스님에 대하여

26 믿는 만큼 行한 만큼

CONTENTS

11   Foreword

13   About Daehaeng Kun Sunim

27   Faith in Action:
        Learning to Rely upon Our Root

공놀이나 하여보세

음지 양지 없는 땅에
뿌리 없는 나뭇잎은
시방 삼계에 스스로
서신 전하여 알려 주며,
메아리도 없고
말도 없는 빈 골짜기에
한 기를 돌려 기둥 세워
공놀이나 하여 보세.

깜짝할 새 오는 것을
깜짝할 새 막으리라.
깜짝할 새 오는 것을
깜짝할 새 막으리라.

-대행큰스님 게송 중에서

Playing with Emptiness

In the land that has neither shade nor sun,
the leaves of the rootless tree
spread the message throughout all realms.
In this empty valley,
where there are no words
and no echoes,
let's set a good foundation
and raise the pillar,
let's play with emptiness.

In the blink of an eye,
things to come can be prevented.
In the blink of an eye,
things to come can be prevented.

– Daehaeng

머리글

대행큰스님이 지난 50여 년 동안 끊임없이 중생들에게 베풀어 주신 수많은 법문이 있었지만, 핵심을 짚어 내는 하나의 단어가 있다면, 그건 아마도 "참나"일 것입니다. 항상 나와 함께 있어서 보지 못하는 내 안의 진짜 나, 그 "참나"를 발견하여 당당하고 싱그럽게 살아가기를 바라는, 중생을 위한 스님의 간절한 바람은 이 한 편의 법문 속에도 여지없이 드러나 있습니다.

누구에게나 내면에는 만물만생을 다 먹여 살리고도 되남는 마음속 한 점의 불씨가 있습니다. 그 영원한 불씨를 찾아 광대무변한 마음법의 이치를 체득하여, 진정한 자유인으로서, 우주의 한 일원으로서 당당히 그 역할을 해 나가길 바라는 대행큰스님의 간곡한 뜻이 이 법문을 통해 여러분 모두의 마음에 전해지길 바랍니다.

한마음국제문화원 일동 합장

Foreword

Over the last fifty years, Daehaeng Kun Sunim gave countless Dharma talks and teachings to beings without number, but if all those talks could be summed up into one word, it would be "true self."

This true essence has always been with us, yet remains unseen. Discover it for yourself, and in doing so, learn to live with courage, dignity, and joy. That all beings should awaken to this true essence is Daehaeng Kun Sunim's deepest wish. When you've tasted the most refreshing spring water imaginable, you naturally want to share it with others.

Within us all is this seed, this spark that feeds and sustains each and every being. Discover this eternal spark and realize its profound and unlimited ability. If you can do this, you'll know what it means to truly be a free person, and you can fulfill the great role that is yours as a member of the whole universe.

With palms together,
The Hanmaum International Culture Institute

대행큰스님에 대하여

　대행큰스님께서는 여러 면에서 매우 보기 드문 선사(禪師)셨다. 무엇보다 선사라면 당연히 비구 스님을 떠올리는 전통 속에서 여성으로서 선사가 되셨으며, 비구 스님들을 제자로 두었던 유일한 비구니 스님이셨고, 노년층 여성이 주된 신도계층을 이루었던 한국 불교에 젊은 세대의 청장년층 남녀들을 대거 참여하게 만들어 한국불교에 새로운 풍격(風格)을 일으키는 데 일조한 큰 스승이셨다. 또한 전통 비구니 강원과 비구니 종단에 대한 지속적인 지원을 펼치심으로써 비구니 승단을 발전시키는 데 중추적인 역할을 하셨다.

　큰스님께서는 어느 누구나 마음수행을 통해 깨달을 수 있음을 강조하시면서 삭발제자와 유발제자를 가리지 않고 법을 구하는 이들에게는 모두 똑같이 가르침을 주셨다.

　스님은 1927년 서울에서 태어나 일찍이 9세경에 자성을 밝히셨고 당신이 증득(證得)하신

About Daehaeng Kun Sunim

Daehaeng *Kun Sunim*[1](1927-2012) was a rare teacher in Korea: a female *Seon(Zen)*[2] master, a nun whose students also included monks, and a teacher who helped revitalize Korean Buddhism by dramatically increasing the participation of young people and men.

She broke out of traditional models of spiritual practice to teach in such a way that allowed anyone to practice and awaken, making laypeople a particular focus of her efforts. At

---

1. Sunim / Kun Sunim: Sunim is the respectful title of address for a Buddhist monk or nun in Korea, and Kun Sunim is the title given to outstanding nuns or monks.

2. Seon(禪)(Chan, Zen)**:** Seon describes the unshakeable state where one has firm faith in their inherent foundation, their Buddha-nature, and so returns everything they encounter back to this fundamental mind. It also means letting go of "I," "me," and "mine" throughout one's daily life.

바를 완성하기 위해 오랫동안 산중에서 수행하셨다. 훗날, 누더기가 다 된 해진 옷을 걸치고 손에 주어지는 것만을 먹으며 지냈던 그 당시를 회상하며 스님은 의도적으로 고행을 하고자 했던 것이 아니라 당신에게 주어진 환경이 그러했노라고, 또한 근본 불성자리에 일체를 맡기고 그 맡긴 일이 어떻게 작용하는지를 관하는 일에 완전히 몰두하고 있었기에 다른 것에는 신경을 쓸 틈이 없었노라고 말씀하셨다.

그 시절의 체험이 스님의 가르치는 방식을 형성하는 데 깊은 영향을 미쳤다. 스님은 우리가 본래부터 어마어마한 잠재력을, 무궁무진한 에너지와 지혜를 가지고 있는데도 대부분이 그 역량을 알지 못해 끊임없이 많은 고통을 겪으며 살고 있음을 절실히 느끼며 안타까워하셨다. 우리들 각자 안에 존재하는 이 위대한 빛을 명백히 알고 있었기에, 스님은 본래부터 가지고 있는 근본자성(自性)인 '참나'를 믿고 의지해 살라 가르치셨고, 이 중요한 진리에서 벗어나는 그 어떤 것도 가르치기를 단호히 거부하셨다.

의도한 바는 아니셨지만, 스님은 매일매일의 일상 속에서 누구나 내면에 갖추어 가지고 있는

the same time, she was a major force for the advancement of *Bhikkunis*,[3] heavily supporting traditional nuns' colleges as well as the modern Bhikkuni Council of Korea.

Born in Seoul, Korea, she awakened when she was around eight years old and spent the years that followed learning to put her understanding into practice. For years, she wandered the mountains of Korea, wearing ragged clothes and eating only what was at hand. Later, she explained that she hadn't been pursuing some type of asceticism; rather, she was just completely absorbed in entrusting everything to her fundamental *Buddha*[4] essence and observing how that affected her life.

---

3. Bhikkunis: Female sunims who are fully ordained are called Bhikkuni(比丘尼) sunims, while male sunims who are fully ordained are called Bhikku(比丘) sunims. This can also be a polite way of indicating male or female sunims.

4. Buddha: In this text, "Buddha" and "Bodhisattva" are capitalized out of respect, because these represent the essence and function of the enlightened mind. "The Buddha" always refers to Sakyamuni Buddha.

근본이자 진수(眞髓)인 참나와 진정으로 통할 수 있게 되었을 때 어떠한 일이 일어나는지를 역력히 보여 주셨다. 사람들은 스님 곁에 있을 때 자신들을 무한히 받아 주고 품어 주는 것만 같은, 말로 형언키 어려운 정밀(靜謐)한 기운을 느꼈고, 스님이 다른 사람들을 도와줄 때 드러내 보이는 깊은 법력 또한 목도하곤 하였다. 하지만 이 모든 일들은 당신 자신을 돋보이게 하거나 과시하려 했던 게 아니었다. 사실 스님께서는 당신의 법력을 늘 감추려고 하셨다. 마음공부의 목적이 놀라운 능력을 갖게 되는 것이 아님에도 대중들이 그것에만 집착하게 되는 폐단을 우려하셨기 때문이었다.

그렇지만 당신이 하신 모든 일을 통해, 우리가 내면에 있는 근본과 진정으로 하나가 되었을 때 그 능력과 자유로움이 어떤 것인지를 보여 주셨다. 스님은 우리 모두가 근본을 통해 연결되어 있으므로 다 통할 수 있고, 그럼으로써 서로 깊이 이해할 수 있다는 것을 보여 주셨으며, 더 나아가 우리가 근본자리에서 일으키는 한생각이 이 세상에 법이 되어 돌아갈 수 있다는 것도 보여 주셨다.

Those years profoundly shaped Kun Sunim's later teaching style; she intimately knew the great potential, energy, and wisdom inherent within each of us, and recognized that most of the people she encountered suffered because they didn't realize this about themselves. Seeing clearly the great light in every individual, she taught people to rely upon this inherent foundation, and refused to teach anything that distracted from this most important truth.

Without any particular intention to do so, Daehaeng Kun Sunim demonstrated on a daily basis the freedom and ability that arises when we truly connect with this fundamental essence inherent within us. The sense of acceptance and connection people felt from being around her, as well as the abilities she manifested, weren't things she was trying to show off. In fact, she usually tried to hide them because people would tend to cling to these, without realizing that chasing after them cannot lead to either freedom or awakening.

어떤 의미에서는 이 모든 일이 우리가 만물만생과 정말로 하나가 되었을 때 자연스레 부수적으로 나오는 것이라고 할 수 있다. 상대를 둘로 보거나 방해물로 여기는 마음이 사라졌을 때, 진정으로 모두와 조화롭게 흘러갈 수 있게 되었을 때 이 모든 일이 가능할 수 있게 되는 것이다. 이렇게 되면, 다가오는 상대가 누구든 별개의 존재로 느끼지 않게 된다. 그들이 또 다른 우리 자신들의 모습이기 때문이다. 일체가 둘이 아님을 뼛속 깊이 느끼는 사람이, 어찌 자신 앞에 닥친 인연을 나 몰라라 하고 등져 버릴 수 있겠는가?

스님은 중생들이 가지고 오는 어려운 문제나 상황들을 해결할 수 있도록 도와 주셨으며, 이러한 스님의 자비로운 원력은 당신이 도시로 나와 본격적으로 대중들을 가르치기 이전에 이미 한국에서는 전설이 되어 있었다. 1950년대 말경, 치악산 상원사 근처 한 움막에서 수행차 몇 년간 머무르신 적이 있었는데, 그 소문을 듣고 전국에서 찾아오는 사람들이 끊이질 않았다. 차마 그들의 고통스런 호소를 내칠 수가 없었던 스님은 일일이 그들의 말에 귀기울이며 마음을

Nonetheless, in her very life, in everything she did, she demonstrated the freedom and ability that arises when we truly connect with this very basic, fundamental essence that we all have – that we are. She showed that because we are all interconnected, we can deeply understand what's going on with others, and that the intentions we give rise to can manifest and function in the world.

All of these are in a sense side effects, things that arise naturally when we are truly one with everyone and everything around us. They happen because we are able to flow in harmony with our world, with no dualistic views or attachments to get in the way. At this point, other beings are not cut off from us; they are another shape of ourselves. Who, feeling this to their very bones, could turn their back on others?

It was this deep compassion that made her a legend in Korea long before she formally started teaching. She was known for having the spiritual power to help people in all circumstances and with every kind of problem. She compared compassion to freeing a fish from a drying

다해 그들을 도와 주셨다. 스님은 자비를 물 마른 웅덩이에서 죽어 가는 물고기를 살리는 방생에 비유하셨다. 집세가 없어 셋집에서 쫓겨난 사람들에게 집을 마련해 주고, 학비가 없어서 학교를 마칠 수 없는 학생들에게 학비를 대주셨지만, 스님의 자비행(慈悲行)을 아는 사람은 손에 꼽을 정도밖에 되지 않았다.

그러나 문제를 해결해 주면 그때뿐 또 다른 문제가 닥쳐오면 속수무책이 되어 버리고 마는 사람들을 보며, 스님께서는 중생들이 자신의 문제를 스스로 해결하고 윤회(輪廻)[1]의 굴레에서 벗어나 자유인이 될 수 있는 도리를 가르치는 일이 더 시급함을 느끼셨다. 누구나가 다 가지고 있는 '참나', 이 내면의 밝디밝은 진수(眞髓)를 알게 하여, 자신들이 자유롭게 사는 것은 물론이요, 자신들의 삶이 인연 맺은 모든 이에게 축복이 되어 이 한세상을 활달히 살아갈 수 있도록 해야겠다고 다짐하셨다.

---

1. 윤회(輪廻): 산스크리트의 삼사라(samsara)를 번역한 말로 쉼 없이 돈다는 생사의 바퀴를 뜻함. 다시 말해, 수레바퀴가 끊임없이 구르는 것과 같이, 중생이 번뇌와 업에 의하여 삼계(三界: 색계, 욕계, 무색계) 육도(六道: 지옥, 아귀, 축생, 아수라, 인간, 천상)라는 생사의 세계를 그치지 않고 돌고 도는 현상을 일컬음.

puddle, putting a homeless family into a home, or providing the school fees that would allow a student to finish high school. And when she did things like this, and more, few knew that she was behind it.

Her compassion was also unconditional. She would offer what help she could to individuals and organizations, whether they be Christian or Buddhist, a private organization or governmental. She would help nun's temples that had no relationship with her temple, Christian organizations that helped look after children living on their own, city-run projects to help care for the elderly, and much, much more. Yet, even when she provided material support, always there was the deep, unseen aid she offered through this connection we all share.

However, she saw that ultimately, for people to live freely and go forward in the world as a blessing to all around them, they needed to know about this bright essence that is within each of us.

마침내 산에서 내려온 스님께서는 1972년 경기도 안양에 한마음선원을 설립하셨다. 이후 40여 년 동안 한마음선원에 주석하시며, 지혜를 원하는 자에게 지혜를, 배고프고 가난한 자에게는 먹을 것과 물질을, 아파하는 자에게는 치유의 방편을 내어 주시는 무한량의 자비를 베푸시며 불법의 진리를 가르쳐 주셨다. 스님은 도움이 필요한 다양한 사회복지 프로그램을 후원하셨고, 6개국에 10개의 해외지원과 국내 15개의 지원을 세우셨다. 또한 스님의 가르침은 영어, 독어, 스페인어, 러시아어, 중국어, 일본어, 불어, 이태리어, 베트남어, 인도네시아어, 아랍어 등으로 번역 출간되었다. 스님은 2012년 5월 22일 0시, 세납 86세로 입적하셨으며, 법랍 63세셨다.

To help people discover this for themselves, she founded the first *Hanmaum*[5] Seon Center in 1972. For the next forty years she gave wisdom to those who needed wisdom, food and money to those who were poor and hungry, and compassion to those who were hurting.

---

5. Hanmaum[han-ma-um]**:** "Han" means one, great, and combined, while "maum" means mind, as well as heart, and together they mean everything combined and connected as one. What is called "Hanmaum" is intangible, unseen, and transcends time and space. It has no beginning or end, and is sometimes called our fundamental mind. It also means the mind of all beings and everything in the universe connected and working together as one. In English, we usually translate this as "one mind."

본 저서는 대행큰스님의 법문을
한국어와 영어 합본 시리즈로 출간하는
〈생활 속의 참선수행〉시리즈 제13권으로
1995년 7월 16일 정기법회 때 설하신 내용을
재편집한 것입니다. 몇 개의 질문은 다른 법문에서
발췌해 추가하였습니다.

This Dharma talk was given by
Daehaeng Kun Sunim on Sunday, July 16, 1995, with
some questions added from other talks.
This is Volume 13 in the ongoing series,
Practice in Daily Life.

Daehaeng Kun Sunim founded ten overseas branches of Hanmaum Seon Center, and her teachings have been translated into twelve different languages to date: English, German, Russian, Chinese, French, Spanish, Indonesian, Italian, Japanese, Vietnamese, Estonian, and Arabic, in addition to the original Korean. For more information about these or the overseas centers, please see the back of this book.

믿는 만큼 行한 만큼

1995년 7월 16일

요즈음 장마철이라 비가 많이 와서 어쩌나 하는 생각을 했습니다. 새벽에 일어나 보니 오늘도 여전히 비가 와서 말입니다. 그런데 다행히 여러분들이 마음[2]을 많이 내신 덕분인지 지금은 이렇게 비를 안 맞게 됐네요.

어떤 분들이 말씀하시기를, "스님께서는 왜 용(用)만 가르칩니까?" 합니다. 그런데 용이라는 것은 우리가 발전하든 안 하든, 우주와 더불어 우리 세상이 그대로 시공을 초월해서 움직이고 있는 그 자체를 이야기한다는 것을 아셔야 합니다.

---

2. 마음(心): 단순히 두뇌를 통한 정신활동이나 지성을 일컫는 말이 아니라, 만물만생이 지니고 있으며, 일체 만법을 움직이게 하는 천지의 근본을 뜻함. '안에 있다, 밖에 있다.' 혹은, '이거다 저거다'라고 말할 수 없으며 시작과 끝이 없고 사라질 수도 파괴될 수도 없음. 시공을 초월하여 존재함.

Faith in Action:
Learning to Rely upon Our Root

July 16, 1995

When I woke up this morning and heard the rain pouring down, I was worried about the people who would be sitting outside listening to the Dharma talk.[6] However, the rain has since stopped and I think it's because so many of you raised a sincere intention that it should.

Someone asked me, "Why are you only teaching people about using spiritual practice to solve problems in their daily life?"[7] Right? You've probably all heard something like this.

---

6. When Daehaeng Kun Sunim gave Dharma talks, it wasn't unusual for 5,000 or more people to attend. Because there weren't enough seats inside, many had to sit outside, listening to the talk through speakers.

7. There is a nuance of criticism for not focusing on "lofty" topics such as the sutras or "enlightenment."

움직이는 자체, 즉 보고, 듣고, 움직이고 하는 자체가 '용'이라는 것입니다. 이 세상에서 움직이며 살고 있는 그것 빼고 뭐가 있습니까? 살면서 내 마음으로 나의 일거수일투족을 다스리고 나가는 그런 것도 모두가 용이요, 보고 듣고 하면서 더 발전하고자 하는 마음을 내는 것도 용이죠. 그러면서 더 나아지는 거죠. 그러니 모두가 '용'이 아니라면 발전이 없습니다. 목석입니다.

반야[3]심경에 이런 구절이 있죠. "색(色)이 공(空)이고, 공(空)이 색(色)이다." 이 말은 그 가운데 고정됨이 없기 때문에 움직이는 사이 없이 움직인다는 뜻입니다. 우리가 지금 배우는 것이 뭐냐 하면, 이 움직임이 없이 움직이는 도리입니다.

---

3. 반야(般若): 대승불교에서 온갖 분별과 망상에서 벗어나 만물의 참다운 실상을 깨닫고 불법의 이치를 꿰뚫어 성불에 이르게 되는 지혜를 뜻함.

However, the act of seeing something, hearing something, moving your body – all of this is the functioning of your foundation, your Buddha-nature. All of the interactions, all of the movement of everything in this world, including the universe itself, is the functioning of our foundation. There's no place this isn't true, and there's no time this hasn't been true.

So, when we try to shape and moderate our ordinary activities by relying upon our foundation, this itself is spiritual practice. When you respond to what you're seeing and hearing by giving rise to a wise thought and entrusting it to your foundation, this too is spiritual development. If we were to ignore the functioning of our fundamental mind as it fills the world around us, how could any growth be possible?

The *Heart Sutra* says, "Form is emptiness, emptiness is form," doesn't it? This is what we've just been talking about: that everything is an interconnected whole, constantly flowing, where nothing remains fixed or unchanging. We are here today to learn this, and how we can apply this truth to our lives.

여러분들이 지금 한시도, 일분일초도 쉬지 않고 움직이시면서 눈을 깜박거립니다. 눈 하나 깜박거리는 것도 용입니다. 우리가, 생명이 살아 있지 않다면, 눈도 깜박거릴 수가 없습니다. 살아 있는 자체가 그대로 용입니다. 흔히들 용신(龍神)을 이야기할 때 모습이 용(龍) 같아서 그러는 줄 아는데, 사실은 찰나에 고정됨이 없이 돌아가는 까닭에 용신(用神)이라 하는 겁니다. 그런데 이렇게 움직이는 도리를 우리가 일일이 이론으로 따지려고 든다면 이 공부는 절대 못합니다.

우리 인간은 우주와 더불어 살아가기에, 우주의 근본과 직결돼 있는 생명의 근본이 있습니다. 그 근본을 불성이라고도 하죠. 이 불성의 에너지는 우주를 덮고도 남습니다. 또 불성의 에너지는 혼자의 에너지가 아닙니다. 불성이라는 것은 바로 우주와 더불어 직결이 돼 있기 때문에 우주의 에너지와도 직결이 돼 있습니다. 그러니 세상하고는 모두 가설이 돼 있는 거와 같습니다.

Right now, everything in your bodies is ceaselessly moving, and there's not a single part of this that isn't the functioning of your inherent nature. Even the blink of your eye is the functioning of your inherent nature. Living and breathing itself are the functioning of this nature. Because the Korean word for "functioning" also sounds like the word for "Dragon," people used the idea of "The Dragon Spirit" to represent the great power that comes from this ceaseless manifesting. Yet if you take this flowing and moving whole, and try to understand it through your own fixed ideas and opinions, how could you make the least bit of progress in your practice?

We are able to live together as one with the universe because the foundation of our life is connected to the foundation of the universe. This is the source of life that exists within each of us. We can call this our essence, or our foundation, or our Buddha-nature, whatever you like. It isn't something that belongs to only a particular individual; rather, it flows through everything in the universe, and through it, all things and lives are connected. There's nothing that isn't part of this.

내가 이런 말을 가끔 하죠? "전력 하나를 가지고 수만 개로 화해서 나투면서 진화되며 돌아간다."라고 말입니다. 이 불성이라는 에너지로 인하여 허공 중에서도 수많은 것들이 바뀌고 발전해 나간다 이겁니다. 비도, 눈도, 바람도 이 모든 절차를 거쳐 거기에서 다 나옵니다.

그러면 인간으로서 우리는 어떻게 해야만 자유스럽게 발전을 할 수 있을까요? 이런 간절한 마음이 있으니 우리가 도반[4]으로서 이 공부를 같이 하는 겁니다. 부처님께서도 당시에 그렇게 가르치셨어요. 어떠한 걸 일일이 따지다 보면 하나도 얻을 수도 발전할 수도 없다고 말입니다.

경에는 화엄경, 법화경, 천수경, 금강경 등이 있고, 그 주요 내용이 함축돼 들어가 있는 반야심경도 있습니다. 세상엔 이렇게 읽을 경들이 많지만, 그 가르침은 하나에서 나왔습니다. 만물만생이 근본을 통해 나왔고 근본을 통해 하나로 돌아간다는 겁니다. 그런데 우리가 생활상에서 벌어지는 모든 일들을 따로 보고 일일이 요거는 요렇고 저거는 저렇고 해 가며 따진다면, 이 마음법은 언제 배웁니까?

---

4. 도반(道伴): 함께 도(道)를 닦는 벗

It's like how electric current can be split apart and transformed, and used in a thousand different ways to make our world a better place. Even in the air, even in the sky, things are changing and transforming through the energy of this Buddha-nature. Rain, snow, and wind all arise through this process.

We've gathered here today, as Dharma brothers and sisters, to learn how to make use of this fundamental energy and free ourselves. This is what the Buddha taught. But he also cautioned that if you get lost in analyzing things that inherently can't be split apart, you won't attain anything, nor will you be able to grow and develop.

There are a lot of sutras, aren't there? Such as the *Flower Ornament Sutra*, the *Lotus Sutra*, the *Thousand Hands Sutra*, and the *Heart Sutra*, which itself includes the deep meaning of all the other sutras. But the many things these sutras teach all arise from the same fundamental truth. It's all descriptions of the same thing. So, if we try to label or define everything in our daily life, as if they were separate things, how could we ever learn about this always-flowing foundation?

아버지 노릇 할 때는 어떻고, 남편 노릇 할 때는 어떻고, 형제 노릇 할 때는 어떻고 해 가며 따진다면 자연스럽게 돌아가겠습니까? 한마음[5]에서 모두가 찰나찰나 바뀌면서 돌아가는 것인데 말입니다.

이 모든 게 하나로 돌아가는 그 부처의 자리도 그 마음에서 나온 것이고, 그러한 헤아릴 수 없는 마음을 낼 수 있으니 부처인 것입니다. 헤아릴 수 없이 볼 수 있기 때문에 부처이며, 헤아릴 수 없이 듣기 때문에 부처인 것입니다. 또 그러한 마음이 있어 우리가 헤아릴 수 없이 응신이 돼서 나투기 때문에 부처인 것입니다. 수없는 나툼에 만물을 진화시키는 그 묘용함이 얼마나 찬란한지 모릅니다. 연기법(緣起法), 연기법 하지마는 여러분들이 진짜로 해 보지 못한다면 그 오묘함을 알 수 없습니다.

---

5. 한마음: '한'이란 광대무변함, 일체가 하나로 합쳐진 것을 뜻하며, 한마음이란 만질 수도 없고 보이지도 않으며, 시공간을 초월하여, 시작도 끝도 없는 근본마음을 말함. 또한, 만물만생의 마음이 삼천대천세계와 서로 연결되어 하나로 돌아가는 것을 의미하기도 함. 다시 말해, 한마음은 우주 전체와 그 속에서 살고 있는 일체 생명들이 근본을 통해 서로 연결되어 그 마음들이 하나로 돌아가는 모든 작용을 포함하고 있음.

If you have a family, then you find yourself naturally switching between the role of a father, to a husband, to a brother, don't you? This is the way our fundamental *one mind*[8] functions – ceaselessly manifesting and changing according to needs and circumstances.

This one mind, which can also be called Buddha, is within us, and is what enables everything to function together. Because this mind within us can give rise to intentions that are subtle and profound beyond imagining, it can be called Buddha. Because this mind can give rise to intentions beyond number, it is Buddha. Because this mind can see and hear anything, it is Buddha. Because of this mind, we are able to respond and manifest in any form needed, and so we are Buddha.

---

8. One mind: (Hanmaum [han-ma-um]) From the Korean, where "one" has a nuance of great and combined, while "mind" is more than intellect and includes "heart" as well. Together, they mean everything combined and connected as one. What is called "one mind" is intangible, unseen, and transcends time and space. It has no beginning or end, and is sometimes called our fundamental mind. It also means the mind of all beings and everything in the universe connected and working together as one.

연기법이라는 이름만 들었지 실천을 한 번도 해 보지 못한다면 무슨 뜻인지조차 도무지 실감이 나지 않습니다.

그러나 알고 보면 우리가 본래 그렇게 할 수 있게끔 돼 있기 때문에 아주 어려운 것은 아닙니다. 할 수 없는 이유는 여러분들이 여러분 자신을 못 믿기 때문이고 여러분들이 여러분 자신을 무시하기 때문입니다. 즉 말하자면 콩 싹이 콩 씨를 무시하는 것과 같습니다.

여러분, 콩 싹은 머지않아서 없어질 텐데도 불구하고 콩 씨를 무시한다면 어떻게 하겠습니까? 콩 씨라는 것은 영원한 것입니다. 내가 콩 씨라고 했다고 해서 또 콩 씨로만 생각하지 마세요. 인간의 근본 종자를 비유해서 말하는 것이니까요. 하지만 실제 콩 씨와 비교를 한다고 해도 그게 맞습니다. 심어서 먹이고, 다 먹고 나면 콩 씨가 나니 그걸 심어서 또 먹이고 말입니다. 그래서 콩 씨 하나 가지고 일체중생들을 다 먹이고도 콩 씨 하나가 되남는다고 하는 겁니다.

This ability to manifest and help beings evolve is so wondrous! Those who haven't experienced the amazing and beautiful ability of mind, those who haven't applied this ability and experienced its results, can't yet truly understand what's represented by ideas such as "*interdependent arising*."[9]

Nevertheless, because we are inherently endowed with these abilities, it's actually not that hard to make use of them. The reason people can't freely use them is because they're ignoring their true self. They don't have faith in it.

It's like a bean sprout ignoring the seed it's growing out of. Does it make sense for the transient sprout to ignore its source? That seed is eternal. I'm not talking about just bean seeds; this is true of the fundamental essence of all life, which is inherent within each of us. Yet, it's also true that the two have something in common. With just one bean seed, you can feed countless

---

9. Interdependent arising, also known as **dependent arising:** The idea that all things arise according to, or dependent upon, other things.

그와 같이 우리의 불성 에너지는 영원한 것이고, 늘지도 줄지도 않습니다. 우리 인간들이 다 죽는다 하더라도 그 불성의 에너지는 그대로 영원합니다. 왜냐하면, 몸을 가지고 태어나 살다 죽는 우리 사람이나 중생들의 생명만 생명이 아니라 전체가 생명이기 때문입니다. 바람도 생명이요, 비도 생명이요, 물도 생명이요, 눈도 생명이요, 이 모든 것이 생명이기 때문입니다.

만물만생의 불성 에너지는 서로 연결되어 같이 돌아가고 있습니다. 그렇지 않다면 이 허공의 에너지가 어디로부터 이렇게 광대하게 나오며, 이렇게 광대하게 생명들을 살리며, 이렇게 광대하게 천차만별로 화해서 바꾸어지면서 찬란하게 꿈을 키우겠습니까.

people, and still have seeds left over to feed people going forward, forever.

Similarly, this energy within us, this Buddha-nature, is eternal – it doesn't increase or decrease. Even if the entire human race died off, this energy wouldn't disappear. Although we die and that energy scatters, it isn't destroyed; it just scatters and then gathers together again, giving rise to other life. It gives rise to beings with bodies, and it gives rise to the wind, for that, too, is alive. Rain is alive, snow is alive, and flowing water, too, is a form of life.

All things are alive with this energy, and through it all the different manifestations that fill this world are connected and function together as a whole. This energy, this power, bursts forth with such infinite and incredible ability, and enables all life to grow and develop in so many different ways. It's this power that enables us to reach our ultimate goal.

Although everyone has this great energy and ability, many of you tend to think of yourselves as powerless, or that you can't do things well, or that you deserve to suffer because of the things you've

그런데 여러분들은 이러한 광대한 능력을 가진 자기에 대해서 어떻게 생각하느냐면은 '나는 무기력하고, 나는 죄가 많다. 나는 업보가 많고, 잘못한 게 많다. 그러니 나는 참회해야만 되고, 기도해야만 되고, 백팔 배 해야만 되고, 삼천 배 해야만 되고....' 이런 식으로 생각을 하십니다. 바로 이러한 지나친 생각 때문에 자기의 모든 능력이 막아지는 겁니다. 자기 마음으로 자기의 능력을 다 막아 놓고는 자기가 뛸려고 그러면 뛰어집니까?

그러니 우리는 이 공부를 필연적으로 해야 합니다. 어찌저찌해서 한번 인간으로 태어났다면, 이 도리를 꼭 알고 가야 됩니다. 그래야 계속 진화할 여건이 되는 겁니다. 이 도리를 알고 가지 않는다면 하위 동물과 다를 게 뭐 있겠습니까?

또 이차적으로는, 여러분이 만약 이 도리를 만났다면 믿고 행해야 된다는 사실을 꼭 아셔야 합니다. 그래야 내 몸과 내 마음을 건강하게 해 줄 뿐만 아니라 크게 나를 발전시키면서 내가 움죽거리는 하나하나가 빛이 되어 남도 도울 수 있기 때문이죠.

done. So instead of using this infinite ability within you, you think you have to go off and bow or chant in proportion to your misdeeds.

However, these kinds of thoughts are actually blocking you. They prevent you from using your own inherent ability. If you're using your own mind to block your ability, do you think you'll be able to grow and evolve? No!

Above all else, you have to know your fundamental mind, and how to make use of it! You've made it to the level of a human being, so don't dare finish this life without knowing this. Then you can keep evolving. If people ignore their fundamental mind and just try to live without awakening to it, how are they different from animals?

Secondly, once you know about your fundamental mind, you need to have faith in its ability and try to apply that to your daily life. You need to know about this, because it's the only way to maintain the health of your body and your mind, and it's also the only way to take a large step forward in your evolution. This is also how everything you do can become a light for others.

내가 가끔 이런 소리를 해요. 주인이 없다면 당신 집은 빈 것이라고요. 이 마음이 부처인데 거기에 진짜 주처를 두지 않고 바깥으로 끄달리면 그 사람에 한해서는 그 집이 비게 되는 겁니다. 만약에 여러분들이 사는 집들을 싹 비워 놓고 방치해 놨다고 생각해 보세요. 아무나 들락날락거리겠죠. 그것도 집 없는 부랑자들이 들어왔다 나갔다, 들어왔다 나갔다 하면서 치우지도 않고 건사하지도 않게 되니, 그냥 거미줄도 치고, 벌레도 생기고, 좀도 슬고 뭐 이만저만 야단이 아니게 될 겁니다. 결국, 집은 썩어서 허물어지게 되겠죠.

　　그러듯이 내 주처의 내면세계도 주인이 딱 자리를 잡고 앉아 발전을 시키면 좋게 발전이 되지만, 반대로 밖으로 끄달리게 되면 마구 망가지게 됩니다. 뭇 생명들이 자기 안에 있던 악종의 알을 까서 수만 개로 만들어 그 원래의 집은 사라지고, 악종의 집으로 만든단 말입니다. 어떻게 생각하세요? 이 말을 허튼소리로 알지 마세요.

This fundamental mind of yours is Buddha, so looking for Buddha outside yourself is exactly the same as leaving your house empty. Imagine if you've gone out somewhere and left your house unlocked, with the doors wide open. Anybody who wanders by can just go in and help themselves to whatever they want, can't they? They can break things, leave a mess, and basically destroy the place. And with no one there, the house begins to fill with bugs and spider webs, and slowly falls apart.

When you are firmly grounded in your fundamental mind, you can protect and guide the consciousnesses that make up your body so that they all work together harmoniously. But if nobody's there, then what? Harmful life forms will invade your body and begin to multiply, spreading throughout it. Soon your nice house will be no more. This is a very real problem.

All of these problems are what you've input in the past, now manifesting in the present. To change that, you have to entrust it all, everything you encounter and every feeling that arises, to your foundation. As you entrust these, this act

우리가 과거에 살아온 것들이 입력되어 현실에 나오는 것이니 현실에 나오는 것을 내가 근본자리에 되놓으라고 하는 이유는, 그전에도 애기했듯이, 되입력을 하면 앞서 입력되어 있던 것이 없어지기 때문이죠.

그렇게 한다는 것은 주인이 있다는 거고, 다스리는 선장이 있다는 거예요. 몸속에 있는 모든 의식들을 다스리는 주인이 있어서 억제도 하고 절제도 하는 겁니다.

눈으로 보고 귀로 듣고 하면서, 주위 모든 것을 살피며 '이렇게 하면 안 되지!' 하면서 자기의식들이 마음대로 하고자 하는 것들을 강력하게 제어할 수 있는 그런 주인이 있어야 하는 겁니다. 그러한 주인이 없다면 그건 바로 애들을 낳아 놓고, 애들만 집 안에 놔두고선 방치하는 격입니다. 그래서 애들이 아무 데서나 친구들이라고 데리고 들어와 집을 아수라장으로 만들면 어떻게 되겠습니까?

재밌는 이야기 하나 해 드릴게요. 어떤 종류의 두꺼비는 말입니다, 일부러 잡아먹히려 큰 구렁이한테 가서 너불너불 약을 올립니다. 그렇게 약을 올려도 구렁이는 처음엔 안 먹으려고

of letting go and entrusting will erase what was previously input. It's just like how, on a cassette tape, new input erases what was previously recorded there.

This is possible because there's the one in charge within you; the captain who can manage the ship is there. The master of the house is present, and can govern the consciousnesses of the many lives within you.

There has to be the one in charge, who can observe what's going on with those consciousnesses, and, when they go off in a harmful direction, can control and restrain them. If there were no such captain, then it would be like parents abandoning young children at home. Or, think of the problems that might ensue if teenagers brought home all their friends, and then left them alone in the house.

Let me give you an analogy. There's a type of toad that will approach a snake and provoke the snake into eating it. In the beginning, the snake tries its best to not eat the toad, but as it keeps getting teased and harassed, it loses its temper and eats the toad. It does this without

안간힘을 씁니다. 그런데 자꾸 앞에 와서 그 입을 툭툭 치고 약을 올리고 쫓아다니며 며칠씩 그러다 보니까 나중에는 구렁이가 화가 나서 이런저런 계산할 여유도 없이 그냥 덥석 물어 두꺼비를 삼킵니다.

먹지 말아야 한다는 걸 알면서도 화를 못 참는 순간 자기를 다스리지 못하고 자신의 분수를 망각하여 죽게 되는 겁니다. 그로 인해 죽은 그 구렁이의 뼈에서는 마디마디마다 두꺼비가 부화가 돼서 나옵니다.

어떤 한 경우에 대해서만 예를 든 건데 무슨 말을 하는 건지는 다 알아들으시겠죠? 바깥에 있는 악종의 세균 같은 것들이 자꾸 내 몸 안으로 들어오려는 것도 있고, 내 몸 안에서 일어나게 하는 것도 있습니다.

예를 들어, 좀 전의 그 두꺼비처럼 자기가 먹히는 척해 가지고 그쪽에다가 자기 생명체를 부화시킨단 말입니다. 이거 아무렇게나 생각해서는 안 됩니다. 좋은 거든 나쁜 거든 잡아먹고 잘 소화시키는 건강한 군사들한테 가서 일부러 먹히고선 그 몸을 갈취하는 겁니다. 예를 들어 말을 하자니깐 이렇게밖에는 할 수가 없네요.

realizing what is going to happen next, for this is a toad whose eggs will only hatch inside a dead animal. Once swallowed, the toad's poison begins to kill the snake. After the snake dies, the eggs hatch within it, and eventually small toads will crawl out from between the bones of the snake.

The snake actually sensed that it shouldn't eat the toad, but in its anger, the snake lost control and gave in to urges beneath itself. And died as a result.

So, now you probably understand what I mean. This same situation applies to protecting yourself from harmful viruses and bacteria. There are dangerous microbes that are always trying to get into your body, and there are dangerous microbes that are latent within your body.

Like the toad and the snake, these outer microbes approach a healthy body and provoke it so that they can be "swallowed." That's not a perfect description, but it will do. Once absorbed, these viruses, bacteria, and microbes begin to multiply within the body and cause any number of serious illnesses, including even leukemia. Please think about this very carefully.

백혈병이니 뭐니 하는, 병원에서도 고치기 참 어려운 병들이 그런 과정으로 형성되는 경우가 있어요. 이게 얼마나 무서운 도리인 줄 아십니까? 이렇게 생긴 것들은 악성이기 때문에, 자기가 성장하기 위해 온몸의 피를 빨아먹습니다. 발끝과 손끝에서부터 그걸 느낄 수 있습니다.

내 몸에 이런 일이 생기는데 좋은 일은 아니지 않습니까? 자기 분신을 그냥, 가차 없이 팽개쳐 없애 버리는 그러한 망종한 일인데 말입니다. 그러니까 내 몸 안에 주인이 떡하니 버티고 있지 않으면 이렇게 사람으로 한번 태어나기가 극히 어렵고, 사람으로 태어났다면 진짜 사람 되기가 또 극히 어렵고, 진짜 사람이 됐다면 부처 되기가 그렇게 또 극히 어렵다고 하는 겁니다.

'지금 시대가 어떤 시댄데, 이렇게 발전이 되고 그랬는데, 그까짓 게 다 뭐야?' 한다면 콩 싹이 콩 씨를 무시하는 것밖에는 안 됩니다. 자기 몸뚱이가 자기 근본 종자를 무시하는 거죠.

내가 내 고깃덩어리를 믿으라고 그랬습니까? 부처님의 형상을 믿으라고 그랬습니까? 이름을 믿지도 말고 허공을 믿지도 마세요. 자기를

These microbes end up causing people no end of suffering. They often grow and increase by consuming the body's blood, and the symptoms of this are often first felt in the toes and fingertips.

Do I even need to say what a horrible thing it is for someone to just sit back and let this happen? To not bring forth your owner, the one in charge, to look after your body is like taking this noble manifestation of our true nature and just throwing the whole damn thing away! Don't you know how hard it is to be born as a human being? It's so hard, and yet even after having a human body, we still have so much work to do in order to become a true human being, let alone a Buddha.

If what I'm talking about seems unimportant, if you think that it's just old folk religion, then, I have to say, this is you disregarding your essence. It's like a bean sprout trying to ignore the very seed it's growing out of.

I've never told you to put your faith in a Buddha statue, in myself, or in some place up above the clouds, have I? The only thing I ever tell you to believe in is your own true seed – your own inherent Buddha essence, the Buddha within you – which is guiding you at all times.

이끌어 가는 자아 부처, 불성을, 진짜 종자를 믿으라는 겁니다.

자아 부처를 믿다 보면 '저 불상의 형상이 다름 아니라 내 내면의 부처이구나! 내가 보고, 듣고, 움직이며 이렇게 무쌍(無雙)하게 발전하게 하는 그 모든 역할을, 앉아서도 천리만리 행할 수 있다는 걸 알게 하기 위함이구나!'라는 것을 깨닫게 될 겁니다. 그래서 '나'부터 알아야지, 내 종자부터 알아야지 하는 겁니다.

콩 씨를 하나 심으려면 흙과 수분이 필요하죠? 수분 없는 흙에는 싹이 나오지 않으니까요. 또 수분만 있고 흙이 없어도 안 돼요. 그렇게 해서 싹이 나왔는데 여러분들은 과거로 돌아가서 콩 종자를 찾으려고 애를 씁니다. 어디 가서 찾습니까? 콩 종자는 벌써 자기 싹으로 화했는데 말이에요. '과거는 이미 지나갔으니깐 없다.' 하는 뜻이 그런 뜻인 겁니다. 콩이 콩 싹으로 화해서 자기가 됐으니 현재에 있는 거지, 과거에 있는 게 아니다 이런 겁니다.

If you keep maintaining sincere faith in this, then the time will come when you realize that statues are a reminder of the inner essence that is moving us, guiding us, and helping us grow and evolve towards levels that are, as yet, utterly inconceivable to you. It's this true nature that is capable of taking care of anything, regardless of distance. Above all else, you must know this seed for yourself. Think carefully about what it takes for a seed to sprout and grow. It can't sprout if it has soil but no moisture. Nor can it grow if it has water but no soil.

Where can you find that seed once it's sprouted and grown? It's right here, in the tree before you. Nonetheless, people have a tendency to search for something that looks like the past shape of the seed. But that has already transformed into something different. This is what past Seon masters meant when they said, "The past doesn't exist because it's moved on." That seed doesn't exist somewhere else, with some other shape. It has transformed into the tree, which is you, right now.

여러분들은 저보다도 더 많이 배우시고, 저보다도 더 넉넉하시고, 또는 지혜롭고, 이런 여러 가지로 볼 때 정말이지, 본받을 일이 너무 많습니다. 여러분들이 아니었으면 난 배우질 못했어요.

여러분들뿐만 아니라 돌 하나, 풀 한 포기도 내 스승 아닌 게 없습니다. 그러니 만약 여러분들이 불교에 대해 공부를 많이 했더라도 "이 정도면 다 알아. 부처님 법이라면 위로 꼬고, 옆으로 꼬고, 가로 꼬고 해도 난 다 알아." 이렇게 하지 마세요. 여전히 배워야 할 게 많고 주위의 모든 것이 스승입니다.

우리가 이 세상에 나왔기 때문에, 내가 나왔기 때문에 하나를 보고 느끼고, 하나를 보고 잘못된 거를 알고, 하나를 보고 잘된 거를 알고, '내가 이렇게 하면 안 되지.' 하는 생각도 들고, '이렇게 하면 되지.' 하는 생각도 드는 겁니다. 이 상대성 원리가 나로 인해서 생긴 겁니다. 내가 없으면 아무것도 없는데 뭐가 있습니까?

그런데 내가 여러 가지 표현으로 이 도리에 대해 여러분들한테 말씀을 해 드리려고 해도 난 배운 게 그리 많지 않아 말이 유창하지 못합니다.

You are all so impressive to me. You have good educations, lead comfortable lives, and understand how this modern world works. I'm so grateful to every single one of you. Because of you, I've been able to learn so much.

And yet, in this life, even a single blade of grass is our teacher. Even a rock alongside the road is our teacher. So regardless of how long you've practiced, or how much you've studied, don't let yourself fall into the trap of thinking that there's nothing more for you to learn about Buddhism or spiritual practice.

Further, everything you're seeing and experiencing, everything you think is going well or badly – you're able to experience and think about all of those things because you're here, because you were born into this world. If you didn't exist, how could any of those thoughts, feelings, or interactions have existed? Because you are here, all of this other stuff is possible.

I'm trying my best to use different expressions and help you understand this, but I'm not well educated, so I can't always explain things as well as I'd like. But what else can I do? All I can do

즉 말하자면, 지금 현실의 용어로 적당하게 잘 둘러댈 줄을 모릅니다. 그렇지만 어떡합니까? 그저 이걸로 끌어대고, 저걸로 끌어대고 이렇게 해서 설명할 수밖에요. 근근 해 갑니다마는, 그러나 방편의 이름이 중요한 게 아니라 그 이면에 있는 진리에 관한 문제이기 때문에 여러분들이 그걸 잘 파악해 주시길 바랍니다. 이건 진실한 문제입니다.

아까 여러분들한테 내 몸속에서 일어나는 문제들, 바깥에서 들어오는 문제들, 이런 것에 대해 어떻게 대처해 나가는지, 어떻게 굴리면서 어떻게 발전을 해 나가느냐에 대해 얘기했습니다. 생각해 보면 아주 겁나는 일이기도 합니다.

그런데 여러분 중에는 한 번도 그거에 대해선 생각해 본 적 없이 그냥 사는 분들도 많이 있습니다. 나는 그저 될 수 있으면 여러분들에게 이것을 알게 해서 스스로 잘 대처해 나갈 수 있으면 얼마나 좋을까 하는 생각으로 애쓰는 겁니다. 이 도리를 몰라 아픔을 겪는 분들이 많다 보니 어떤 때는 하루에도 몇 번씩 눈시울이 뜨거울 때가 있어요.

is try to explain, using bits and pieces from here and there. Yet ultimately, the terms I use aren't important, they're just a method. You have to do the work to grasp the truth that underlies all of these. I can't tell you how critically important this is.

One of the things I wanted to talk about today is this issue of harmful things – both those coming from outside your body as well as those arising from within it – and how you can handle them and also protect your body, so that you can grow and evolve. When you can see for yourself how these kinds of problems can change the course of a person's life, it's often quite terrifying.

However, most people haven't given the least bit of thought to issues like this. That's why I take every opportunity that I can to tell you how serious this is, and to show you how to take care of these things for yourself. When I see the needless suffering and pain people go through because they don't know this, well, there's a reason my eyes well up with tears several times a day.

생활하면서 많은 일들이 있을 겁니다. 거기에 여러분들 마음의 잣대를 대려 하지 말고, 상대 마음의 잣대를 대서 둥글게, 항상 자비스럽게 마음을 내십시오. 몰라도 깔보지 말고, 알아도 높이 보지 말고 항상 둥글게 해 나가십시오.

우리가, 내가 이 한마음을 쓰는 대로 내 몸속의 그 의식들이 따라갑니다. 여러분들의 마음 씀씀이대로 따라갑니다. 그러기 때문에 한생각[6]하기가 극히 어렵다고 하는 겁니다.

외국에 살던 어떤 분이 그래요. "스님, 제가 여기서 스님을 뵈러 다닐 때는 그걸 몰랐는데 외국에 나가서 외롭다 보니까 스님을 자주 찾게 됩니다. 외국이다 보니 무슨 일이 생기거나, 혹은 학교에서 수업 중에 칠판에다 쓴 거 하나도 의미가 잘 이해되지도 않고 그럴 때는 어떻게 할 수가 없어서 그냥 마음으로 스님을 부릅니다.

---

6. 한생각: 어떤 생각을 우리들 내면의 근본 자리에 입력시키거나 맡겨 놓았을 때, 근본을 통해 나오는 생각은 우리들 몸속의 모든 생명들뿐만 아니라 이 세상의 만물만생에 전달되며, 일체가 그 생각에 응하게 됨. 보이지 않는 정신계, 즉 우리들 근본마음을 통해 일으켜지는 생각은 물질계에서 현실로 나타나게 됨. 이렇게 근본을 통해 나오게 되는 생각을 한생각이라 함.

The thing is, I can't make others behave in accordance with what I know to be the best way forward. All I can do, all any of us can do, is think of others with kindness and compassion, and help guide them according to their own level of understanding. Do this harmoniously, without looking down upon those still lost in ignorance. Also, in the same vein, don't place those who are doing well on a pedestal.

Take care of things in this way because all the lives within your body are acting upon and following your thoughts. They just mirror your generosity – or your narrow-mindedness. This is why it's often so hard to raise thoughts from our foundation. It's something we have to work hard at.

Some people, well, many people actually, have similar experiences of when they began to make this connection with their foundation. One of the members here put it this way.

"Sunim, I really didn't understand how precious this fundamental mind is when I was home in Korea. But when I went overseas, I felt

이거는 뭐 어떻게 할 수가 없어서 그냥 간절한 마음으로 공부하고 갔습니다. 그런데 그러다 보니 어떻게 된 일인지 나도 모르게 그냥, 남보다 떨어지지 않게 그냥 대처해 나가지더라고요."

어느 날, 이 사람이 외국에서 경제적으로 아주 힘들게 살 때 세 들어 살던 조그만 방에 도둑이 들었더랍니다. 그 당시 자신의 처지가 너무 딱하고 힘들어서 그 심정을 종이에 끄적거려 놓았던 게 있었는데 도둑이 그걸 봤나 보더래요. 그 종이 위에다가 오히려 돈을 좀 놓고 갔더랍니다. 너무 기가 막힌 자기의 심정을 눈물을 흘리며 썼던 글이라 그런지 오히려 도둑의 마음도 같은 심정이 됐나 봅니다. 이런 이야기를 편지에 써서 나한테 보내왔는데 "세상에 어떻게 이런 일이 있을 수가 있습니까?"라고 하면서 본인도 그 마음에 감동받았답니다.

so lonely and often called to *Juingong*[10] from the bottom of my heart. Especially when something happened to me, or when I couldn't keep up in class, I had nothing. All I could do was call to Juingong – and you – for help. I would call for help and try desperately hard to entrust all of my problems to this fundamental mind. As I kept doing this, I found myself keeping up with my classes."

There was another episode involving this lady. While she was out, a burglar broke into the room she was renting. She had almost nothing, and as the burglar searched her room, he found a poem that she'd written, describing how hard life was, being so poor and far away from her home country, and how sad she felt. You can't imagine what happened next: When she came home that

---

10. Juingong(主人空)**:** Pronounced "ju-in-gong." Juin (主人) means the true doer or the master, and gong (空) means "empty." Thus Juingong is our true nature, our true essence, the master within that is always changing and manifesting, without a fixed form or shape.

Daehaeng Sunim has compared Juingong to the root of the tree. Our bodies and consciousness are like the branches and leaves, but it is the root that is the source of the tree, and it is the root that sustains the visible tree.

사람이 너무 불 밑에 있으면 그 불빛이 밝은 줄 모르는 것처럼 공부하는 도량에서 다 같이 공부하다가 멀리 떨어져 혼자 있다 보면 그 빛이 얼마나 밝은 줄을 알게 됩니다.

마찬가지로 자기와 자기 콩 씨가, 콩 씨와 콩 싹이 아주 가깝게 붙어 있으니 너무도 좋긴 한데, 도대체 자기 콩 씨가 얼마나 위대한지 모르는 거예요.

한편으론, 이 공부가 웬만큼 돼서 감응이 좀 됐다 싶으면, 어떤 사람은 다시 바깥으로 치우쳐서 단전호흡 같은 것을 해서는 그냥 귀로 환청이 들리고, 머리로 뜨거운 열이 나오고, 몸이 들리고, 온통 야단법석이 납니다. 하지만 꾸준히 내면으로 관(觀)[7]하고 들어가는 사람들한텐 그런 일이 없습니다. 근본과 하나가 되어 내 마음이 발전되니 그런 부작용이 없습니다. 귀로 들리거나 그런 법도 없고요.

---

7. 관(觀): 어의적으로 '관찰하다' '보다'라는 뜻을 가지고 있으며, 마음공부를 하는 과정에서는 '참나'인 주인공을 믿고 맡기는 것을 뜻함. 즉, 삶에서 부딪치는 모든 문제들을 주인공만이 해결할 수 있다는 철저한 믿음으로 주인공에게 맡겨 놓고 분별없이 집착 없이 지켜보는 것을 통틀어 '관'이라 함.

evening, she found her poem on her desk, and folded up inside it was a thousand dollars!

Whoever it was that broke into her room was so moved that instead of stealing from her, he gave her money! She wrote about this to me, calling it a miracle, and still in shock that her foundation could work in such a way. Like the saying goes, when you're standing right next to a lighthouse, you don't realize how bright it is until you move away from it. Then you can appreciate just how bright and wonderful that light is.

This same thing applies to you and your own root. This root is so much a part of us that people don't even see it. Your root is so close to you that once your practice has deepened, you can easily communicate back and forth with it. It's just so amazing. Imagine the feeling of connection that comes from always being in touch with your root and always being able to communicate with it!

Yet there are people who get twisted around and start trying to find something more powerful or dramatic outside of themselves. But those who seek like this, chasing things like ki and such, often end up experiencing all kinds of unpleasant

마음으로 발전이 돼서 자꾸자꾸 스스로 알아지고, 스스로 느껴지고, 스스로 봐지고, 스스로 하게 되고 그러는 겁니다.

이뿐만이 아니라, 우주적인 면으로도 이 공부가 얼마나 대단한 건지 여러분들은 아마 생각조차 못할 겁니다. 모든 사람들이, 그리고 모든 우주의 전체 행성이라든가, 별성, 이 모든 것이 그 자체 그대로만 있는 게 아니에요. 쉼 없이 변하며 자기 생을 살고 있어요.

우리 인간의 수명은 짧지만, 더 긴 수명을 가진 것들도 있고, 또 우리보다 더 짧은 수명을 가진 것들도 많습니다. 생명들이 말입니다. 우린 그보다는 좀 수명이 긴데, 수명이 아주 긴 별성들도 있고, 행성들이 있지만, 우주의 모든 것들이 다 그마다 하나하나의 세계가 있고, 하나하나의 작용이 있고, 하나하나의 그 생이 있단 말입니다.

side effects. They may hear things that aren't there, feel a horrible pressure in their head, or even levitate off the ground. However, those who seek their root by trying to directly entrust it with the stuff that comes up in their everyday life don't experience any of these harmful things.

Instead, a firm awareness of their own root grows within them, and their spiritual practice becomes more and more deep. They become able to answer their own questions, to see for themselves, to feel for themselves, and to respond fully and completely to whatever arises.

Let me talk about something else now. Until you've awakened, you can't possibly imagine the power this practice has to affect even the functioning of the universe. Through your Buddha-nature, you are connected to the Buddha-nature of everything in the universe. Their energy and our energy, our Buddha-nature, are functioning together as one, just one. That is what I mean when I say that our Buddha-nature is connected to the Buddha-nature of the universe. This energy is so huge and incredible, you just can't imagine it.

우리가 우주와 직결이 돼 있다는 것은 우리의 에너지와 우주의 모든 별성들의 에너지가 연결되어 있다는 뜻입니다. 다시 말해, 불성과 불성끼리 하나로 돌아가는 에너지가 광대하게 연결되어 있다는 겁니다.

그래서 여러분들이 정말이지 마음을 기울여 이 공부를 해야 될 이치가 바로 여기에 있는 겁니다. 가만히 보니깐 전 세계를 다 돌아다녀 봐도 즉각적으로 이렇게 내 콩 싹이 콩 씨를 찾는 공부를 하는 사람들이 그렇게 많지 않아요.

전부 밖으로 기도하고, 모두 어떤 상대를 놓고 그것을 믿고, 기도하고 뭔가를 해 달라고 빌고 그러는 거지, 직접 자기 콩 싹이 콩 씨를 근중하게 생각하고 내면세계를 발전시켜 그 중심에서 중용으로써, 벌어지는 일에 가차 없이 대처할 수 있는 능력이 생기게 하는 공부는 하나도 하고 있지 않아요.

Nothing in this universe – not the planets, not the stars – stays still. It is all ceaselessly functioning and performing its own role, and has its own life span. Humans, stars, and bugs all have different life spans and roles, but their Buddha-nature is working together as one. This energy is so magnificent! I desperately wish that people would make spiritual practice something important in their lives, and so awaken to this for themselves.

But when I look around at the world, there are so few people, almost no one, really, trying to connect directly with their own root. It seems like everyone is praying to outside objects. They set up something outside themselves, believe in it, and then beg that for help.

I wish there were more people who realized that their own root is the most important thing of all, and who were focused on how to connect with it and develop this great inner potential.

With this, everyone can take care of any kind of problem they encounter, both things of the visible realm as well as of the unseen realms, and do so with a steady heart.

그러니 내가 생각할 땐 여러분들이라도 공부를 열심히 해서 대처를 할 수 있도록 해야 한다는 겁니다. 그런데 사실 이 공부라는 것도 공부라는 이름을 붙였을 뿐이에요. 무슨 소리 하는지 상대가 알아듣게끔 하기 위해서 그 이름을 붙여 놓은 거지 그 이름은 아무것도 아닙니다. 어쨌든 이것을 공부라고 하든 수행이라고 하든 진실하게 해서 우주적으로 오는 문제까지도 잘 대처해 나갈 수 있어야 합니다.

지금 우리 지구가 태양계에 있다고 해서 여기에서 오는 문제만 생각해선 안 돼요. 은하계며 전체 우주가 서로 연결돼 돌아가기 때문에 서로 간에 문제가 다 결부돼 있습니다. 예를 들어, 태양의 수명이 다 돼서 없어진다든가 팽창된다든가 이런다면 우리 지구에 붙어서 사는 생명체들이 전멸함은 물론이거니와 연결돼 있는 많은 다른 곳의 생명들에게도 치명적인 손실이 가게 됩니다.

So, my hope is that you all will practice this diligently and be able to take care of whatever arises. Even words like "practice" and "study" are just labels, terms we use to communicate. The important thing is that you truly practice relying upon and using this root, this connection, so that you can take care of the problems of the Earth, and even of the Universe itself.

If there's a problem with the Earth, its effects are not going to be limited to just our solar system. Because all aspects of the universe are interconnected, their problems likewise affect each other. For example, if our sun reached the end of its life and either burned out or expanded wildly, life in this solar system would be wiped out, of course. But throughout the universe, there are dimensions and many living beings that have a connection with life on Earth, so the harm to life in those places, too, would be terrible beyond imagining.

There's absolutely nothing that remains motionless and unchanging, not on this Earth, not the Earth itself, nor any single thing in the whole universe. All of it is ceaselessly moving,

현재 지구뿐만 아니라 우주 전체가 다 쉼 없이 운동하고 있습니다. 보이는 세계뿐만 아니라, 불성의 세계, 이 모든 데서 시공을 초월해 돌아가면서 이게 자동적으로 벌어졌다, 오므라졌다 하는 이치가 있기 때문에 이 지구도 그냥 고정되게 가만히 있을 수 없는 겁니다.

이 지구 상에 많은 나라들이 있지만, 만약 여러분들이 살고 있는 이 한국에서 조그마한 일도 아니고 어떠한 큰일이 벌어진다면 어떻게 감당하겠습니까? 한쪽 땅덩어리가 가라앉으면 다른 한쪽에서는 물난리가 나기도 하고 땅이 불쑥 솟아오르기도 합니다. 없어지기도 하고, 기울어지기도 하고, 벌어지기도 하고, 붙기도 하고, 붙을 때 또 그냥 가서 붙는 게 아니라 잘못 어긋나게 붙기도 하고, 화산이 폭발하기도 합니다. 그렇게 시시각각 우리가 움죽거리는 것처럼 지구 자체도 움죽거리고 있는 겁니다.

그러면 이러한 문제들을 잘 대처해 가며 이끌어 나가야 하는데 어떻게 이끌어 갈 것이냐 이겁니다. 부처님 법은 이렇게 한다도 없고, 저렇게 한다도 없습니다. 이 세상은 고정되게 딱 정해져 있는 것이 아무것도 없기 때문입니다.

expanding, and contracting. And not just in the visible realm: the unseen realms and the realm of Buddha-nature are all ceaselessly changing, with time and space counting for nothing.

Suppose some huge disaster was about to happen in Korea; how would you take care of it? What if huge parts of the country were about to sink into the ocean, or high mountains were going to flatten out, or plains were going to rise up to become mountains, or continents were going to merge together or pull apart, causing volcanoes to erupt, and so on? The Earth is constantly changing and moving like this.

How then, can we manage those problems? How can we guide them toward a less harmful outcome? In this interconnected and constantly changing whole, there is no one fixed or "right" way to handle things. Instead, if we firmly ground ourselves in our foundation, our root, then, because we are firmly connected with this whole, the best response for that situation will naturally arise. This, too, is a form of what we call "*Doing without any thought of doing.*" [11]

그러니 대처하는 법도 딱 고정된 게 아니죠. 때마다 다가오는 대로 잘 대처해 나갈 수 있고 그렇게 이끌어 나갈 수 있는 것이 바로 함이 없이 하는 도리이고, 함이 없이 해야만 또 그게 그렇게 잘 돌아가게 되는 겁니다.

우리가 이 세상을 다 주고도 바꿀 수 없는 게 이 공부입니다. '내가 꼭 이거를 한다.' 하고 시작하는 게 부처님 법이 아니라, 내가 힘이 있으면 있는 그대로 그냥 함이 없이 하는 게 이 공부입니다. 자기 근본에 모든 걸 일임해 놓고 물 흐르듯 자연스럽게 대처를 해 나가는 것입니다. 그렇게 흘러가듯 하면 되는데 자기 마음이 괜히 긁어 부스럼을 만들어 놓고 그로 인해 다시 더 아파하는 것은 어쩔 수 없는 거죠.

삼풍백화점이 무너지는 그 난리가 난 것도 바깥으로만 끄달리고 자기 콩 씨를 짐작해 보지도 못했기 때문에 일이 일어난 거예요. 자기 자신을 침착하게 들여다보지 못하고, 자기를 다스리지 못하고, 그 모든 걸 이끌어 주는 주인을 무시했기 때문에 그런 일이 벌어진 거죠.

Nothing in all the world is more valuable than this ability to rely upon our root. Here, in the Buddha's *Dharma*,[12] there is no "I can do it" or "I will do it." When you have the ability to take care of something, you just do it. You respond naturally, entrusting everything to your true nature like the flowing of water, with no "me" or "I did." However, by using their minds unwisely, people often end up creating their own problems. They keep scratching healthy skin, until finally it bleeds.

Take the case of the Sampoong department store disaster;[13] the building collapsed because,

---

11. Doing without any thought of doing: While this can mean thought and action free of any sense of a separate "me" or "I" that's doing things, it also means letting go of the thought that "I" did something or experienced something, once we become aware of that train of thought.

12. Dharma: This refers to both ultimate truth, and the truth taught by the Buddha.

13. Sampoong department store: This was a high-end luxury department store in southern Seoul that collapsed on June 29, 1995, killing 502 people and injuring 937. Its collapse was due to faulty construction, but the death toll was a result of the owners refusing to close the large basement supermarket, despite cracking and booming sounds being heard on the upper floors. They closed the upper floors, but left the supermarket open to take advantage of the late afternoon rush of people preparing for dinner.

그 건물을 짓고 책임 맡은 사람들이 이런 공부하는 분들이었다면, 그 사람들이 진짜로 자기 근본, 자기 콩 씨를 믿는 그런 분들이었다면 그렇게 무너지게 두지는 않았을 거예요. 물론 그런 사람은 애초에 그렇게 무너지게 짓지도 않았겠지만 말예요. 어찌 됐든 만약에 건물의 어느 옆이 잘못됐으면, 그런데 자기가 아직 깨닫지는 못해서 현실에서 인식을 못 하면, 꿈으로라도 그냥 보여 줘요.

예전에 어느 건축업에 종사하시는 한 신도님이 꿈을 꿨는데 꿈에서 누가 "야! 이쪽이 잘못됐으니까 이쪽을 봐봐. 가서 봐봐. 거기를 한번 이렇게 헤치고 봐봐." 이러더랍니다. 하도 이상해서 짓던 건물에 가서 보니까 진짜 어느 기둥 중간 부분에 모래하고 시멘트가 꽉 정체가 돼서 들어가지를 못하고 막혀서 있더랍니다. 그거를 만약에 건물을 다 짓고 나서 알았더라면, 큰일 날 뻔하지 않았습니까? 그런데 그걸 그렇게 알게 돼 해결할 수 있었으니 얼마나 신기한 일입니까? 그분은 아주 탄복을 했답니다.

during construction, everyone from the contractor to the owners were completely absorbed in outer things and didn't give the least bit of thought to the seed within themselves. They couldn't calmly reflect inwardly, and they ignored their true nature, which was trying to lead them in wise directions. Thus, that disaster happened.

If someone in charge had been a practitioner with faith in their own root, then that collapse wouldn't have happened. Of course, such a person wouldn't have cut corners like that in the first place. Anyway, even if that person wasn't awakened and so couldn't truly perceive what was going on, they would still have been given a message in their dreams, at least.

For example, one of the members here worked for a construction company, and one day had a dream where someone called out, "Hey! Something went wrong on this side of the building! Open up that concrete mold and check it out."

So, the next day he went to that side of the building and carefully examined the main concrete support pillars. They looked okay at

우리가 이 공부하는 자체가 뭔지 한번 생각해 보십시오. 사람들은 자기 콩 씨가 콩 싹을 형성시켜서 살고 있는데도 불구하고 콩 싹이 어디서 그냥 나온 것처럼 혼자 산다고 아주 그냥 야단들이거든요. 자기가 혼자 사는 게 뭐 있습니까? 물 한 모금을 먹어도 혼자 먹지 않고 더불어 헤아릴 수 없는 생명들이 서로서로 같이 먹고 사는데 말예요.

　이건 종교적인 가르침에 국한된 게 아니라 과학적이고, 의학적이고, 철학적입니다. 모두 다 연결돼 있습니다. 그래서 선(禪)과 학(學)이 둘이 아닌 겁니다. 몸과 자기 불성도 둘이 아닙니다. 콩 씨와 콩 싹이 둘이 아니듯이 떼려야 뗄 수가 없죠. 콩 싹이 없어도 콩이 없고, 콩이 없어도 콩 싹이 없으니까요.

first glance, but once he started testing them with a hammer, he realized that the several of the pillars were full of air pockets. If that had been discovered after the upper levels were added, they would have had to tear down half the building and begun again. This would have been a huge disaster for his company, so he was thrilled to have found it early, and amazed at how his true nature let him know about it.

Actually, nothing exists apart from our true nature. People are living here right now because their seed gave rise to a sprout. Yet they rush about, thinking they're cut off from everything else. As if a sprout somehow appeared without a seed or a root?! What does it mean to be alive? To drink even one sip of water involves millions of beings working and living together. There is no "you" that lives apart from everything else.

This isn't some religious teaching. It's science, medicine, and philosophy. All things are connected to each other. Meditation and the sutras aren't separate, nor are your body and Buddha-nature separate. None of it can be split apart. You can't have a bean sprout without a

그런데 내가 공부하라고 하면 어떤 사람들은 "아이고, 나는 바빠서 할 새가 없어서 못 합니다." 이러거든요. 하하하. 그럴 때 보면요, 난 저절로 웃음이 나고 아주 죽겠어요.

자기가 태어나서 살아나가는 게 콩 씨가 콩 싹을 형성시켜 나와서 자기가 또 콩 씨를 만드는 건데 시간이 없대요. 글쎄 누가 백일기도를 하랬나, 삼천 배 절을 하랬나. 시간이 좀 여유가 있으면 앉아서 '주인공(主人空)[8], 너만이 너가 있다는 증명을 할 수 있어.' 하고 관하고, 또 그럴 여유도 없으면 그냥 일하면서도 그렇게 관하라는 거죠.

앉으나 서나 화장실에 가나 잠시 잠깐이라도 그렇게 하라는 겁니다. 불법에는 더럽고 깨끗한 게 없으니까, 자기가 있는 그 자리에서 다 그냥 통하는데 뭐가 바빠서 못합니까, 글쎄. 나 참, '바빠서'라뇨.

---

8. 주인공(主人空): 우리 모두 스스로 갖추어 가지고 있는 근본마음으로 일체 만물만생의 근본과 직결된 자리. 나를 존재하게 하고, 나를 움직이게 하며, 내 모든 것을 관장하는 참 주인이므로 주인(主人)이며, 매 순간 쉴 사이 없이 변하고 돌아가 고정된 실체가 없으므로 빌 공(空)자를 써서, 주인공(主人空)이라 함.

bean seed. Without the bean seed, the sprout couldn't exist, and without the bean sprout, there could not have been a bean seed.

And yet people say things to me like, "Oh! I'm so busy, I just don't have time to practice," which is just such a ridiculous idea that I can only laugh out loud. Do you know why? Your life itself is nothing other than the process of a seed becoming a sprout, living its life, and then forming a seed again.

I've never told you to go off and meditate for a hundred days or to go do 3,000 bows, have I? If you happen to have some free time, sit down and ask your true nature to show itself, to give you a sign that it exists. If you're busy, then just do this as you work. Practice like this wherever you are, whatever you're doing, whether you're walking, standing, or sitting on the toilet.

Wherever you are, no matter whether that place is dirty or clean, that's where Buddha exists. Right there, all things and life are connected together and communicating as one.

So it's just absurd to think that you don't have time to practice. There are these kinds of

이렇게 모르는 분들이 있기도 합니다. 바깥으로 끄달리던 공부를 하던 분들은 자기 근본을 믿고 일임하며 안으로 관하기가 그렇게 어렵습니다.

여러분들은 '내가 있으니까 이 모두가 있구나.' 하는 사실을 잊지 마세요. 콩 씨와 콩 싹은 떼려야 뗄 수 없다는 걸 명심하세요. 또 자손들도 그렇습니다. 선업으로 오는 자식들도 있고 악업으로 오는 자식들도 있습니다. 천차만별입니다, 그 자식이 생기는 연유가.

그러니 그런 거에는 신경 쓰지 말고 그저 모든 걸 내 근본에 도로 다 되놓아요. 내 가슴에 홍락을 주든 대못을 박든, 자식과의 문제가 뭐가 됐든, 듣기 싫어하는 말을 자꾸 한다거나 때린다고 되는 게 아니에요. 오히려 더 빗나가요. 너무 속상한 마음에 욕도 하고 때리기라도 하면 그냥 집을 나가 버리기도 합니다. 허허허. 여러분들 참 경험 많이 하실 겁니다.

uninformed people, and there are also people who find it hard to practice because they've been trained to pray outwardly, to seek truth outside of themselves.

Let me move on for now. Please don't forget that everything you're experiencing with other people is happening because you're involved. You can't have a bean sprout without a bean seed there under the soil. This is particularly true when it comes to your children. You meet because of every kind of reason imaginable. Sometimes parents and children meet each other because of the good karma between them, and sometimes they meet because there is evil karma between them.

But don't worry about any of this. No matter whether your kids fill you with joy, or make you feel like they drove a railroad spike through your heart, yelling at them or even hitting them won't make things any better, will it? It only makes things worse. It just makes your children want to run away from home. [Sighs.] A lot of you have probably suffered through things like this.

오랫동안 앉아 있자니 다리 아프시죠? 괜찮으니까 그냥 쭉 뻗으세요. 괜찮습니다.

좀 전에 얘기했듯이 이런 걸 해결할 수 있는 방법은, 내가 있으니 이 모든 게 있다는 걸 아시고, 또, 콩 씨와 콩 싹이 둘이 아닌 것도 알아, 내 안에 모든 걸 다 넣어 하나가 되게 하는 겁니다.

'업이 생기게 된 것도 너고, 업이 안 생기게 하는 것도 너야. 나는 내 근본과 더불어 같이 공했어. 그러니 내 근본과 하나가 될 수 있는 너만이 이 모든 걸 해결할 수 있어.' 그러곤 그냥 딱 거기다가 맡겨 놓고 지켜보기만 하라, 이런 겁니다.

[To the audience, who are sitting cross-legged on cushions in the Dharma hall] Go ahead and stretch out your legs. It's completely okay. You're the only one who can take care of your body. Nobody else can, or will, do it for you.[14]

How should you handle these kinds of family problems? Think back to what I just said: you and your root are inseparable. Everything arises, or not, through the functioning and power of this inherent nature.

So entrust everything back within yourself, reminding yourself that, "It's you, true nature, through which karma can arise, and it's you that can keep it from arising. This flesh I have isn't my foundation, and it isn't my true shape. This 'me' doesn't exist at all. So 'I' don't have to get tangled up in these things. It's you, as the whole, that can take care of all this."

And then, deeply entrust where you are now and what you're facing to this essence, and just keep observing.

---

14. In Korean temples, it's considered rather rude to point the soles of your feet at someone. So in Dharma halls, people are reluctant to stretch out their legs in front of them, towards the Buddha statue or a sunim giving a talk.

개미도 배가 고프면 먹이를 찾아 먹을 줄 아는데 어떻게 사람이 나갔는데 자기 살 궁리 안 하겠습니까? 하지만 부모가 돼 가지고 나 몰라라 하면 안 됩니다.

어떤 부모는 돈만 쥐여 주고 마는 경우도 있는데 그러면 안 돼요. 돈을 번다는 게 얼마나 어려운지도, 얼마나 귀한지도 몰라요. 그러기 때문에 마구 사는 거죠. 그러면 장래가 어떻게 되겠습니까? 그러니까 돈을 주는 것도 너무 적게 줘도 안 되고, 너무 많이 줘도 안 된다 이겁니다. 그리고 그렇게 돈으로만 해결하려고 하지 말고 항상 내 근본에 맡겨 마음으로 같이 불이 들어오게 하세요.

서로의 생활에 관심 없어 보이는 사람들이라도 한집에 같이 사는 식구인데 어찌 아끼는 마음이 없겠습니까? '너의 주인공과 내 주인공이 둘이 아니거늘, 내 마음에 불을 켜면 어찌 너한테는 불이 안 켜지랴. 모두 다 한마음으로써,

Even ants have an innate sense of good judgment and can take care of themselves, so how much more so your children? They still need your attention and guidance of course, but you don't need to be too worried about them.

As you probably know, giving children too much can ruin them. They end up not valuing what they've been given, and have no idea how much effort it takes to earn even a little money. And they often end up leading absurd lives. What kind of a future will such children have? So when you give your children an allowance, you shouldn't give them too much or too little. Just keep entrusting everything between you to this fundamental mind of yours, then as your heart becomes brighter, your child's will, too.

Even though as a family you may not be that interested in each other's pursuits, you still love each other, don't you? Share love with them by entrusting the following thought to your foundation, "Your foundation and mine aren't separate. As the light within me becomes brighter, yours will, too." It's this deep foundation that help us brighten our minds and develop a

밝은 마음으로써, 대처해 나갈 수 있는 '너'가 되게 하는 것도 주인공 바로 너뿐이잖아?' 하고 관하세요. 그게 진짜 사랑입니다.

그렇게 자꾸 관해 준다면 나갔던 놈도 그냥 기를 쓰고 들어올 겁니다, 아마. 이거 거짓말 아닙니다.

여러분들이 어떤 때는 '주인공, 주인공!' 이름만 찾고선 "아휴! 나갔던 사람이 안 들어옵니다." 이러거든요. 또 "아픈 게 잘 낫질 않습니다." 그래요. 내가 의사입니까? 내가 그렇게 고쳐 주는 사람이에요? 여러분 자체에 천차만별로 화해서 돌아가는 한마음이 있는데 어찌 의사는 안 되겠습니까?

warm, healthy relationship. It's this foundation that can lead you toward wise paths.

Entrusting like this is true love. If you keep doing this, even a child who has run away will do everything they can to return home. This is so true.

Some of you only pay lip service to the idea of Juingong, and then come and tell me things like your son hasn't returned home, or a sick person isn't getting any better. What am I, a doctor? No. It's your own Juingong, your true foundation, that can manifest according to your need, so why wouldn't it manifest itself as doctor?

If you are sick, it will become a doctor for you; if you need to live longer, it will become the spirit of the *Northern Dipper*.[15] If you need a guide in the realm of the dead, it will become *Ksitigarbha Bodhisattva*[16] for you. If you are

---

15. The Northern Dipper: (Also known as the Big Dipper.) Traditionally in Korea, people have believed that the seven stars of the Northern Dipper govern the length of humans' lives.

16. Ksitigarbha Bodhisattva(地藏菩薩)**:** The guardian of the earth who is devoted to saving all beings from suffering, and especially those beings lost in the hell realms.

가족이 아프면 의사가 돼 주고, 금방 죽을 것 같으면 칠성이 돼 주고, 좋은 데로 못 갈 것 같으면 지장이 돼 주고, 액난이 닥치면 관세음이 돼 주고, 용신이 돼 주고, 조왕이 돼 주고, 지신이 돼 주고, 다 그렇게 천차만별로 본인이 원하는 대로 될 수가 있는데 뭐가 문제입니까? 단지 여러분 생각이 잘못됐을 뿐이니까 여러분이 알아서 하십시오.

내가 만약에 이 모든 걸 할 줄 알아서 내가 여러분 대신에 해 줬다 하면은 여러분은 아주 구할 길이 없어지는 겁니다. 그런데도 나한테 와서는 그런 걸 바래요. 이런 일들을 수시로 겪고 있습니다. 이것도 고충이라면 고충이겠지요.

desperately poor or in trouble, it will become *Avalokitesvara*[17] for you. If you are at sea and need help, it will become the dragon spirit in order to help you. It will become the kitchen god, the earth spirit, whatever you need.

So then, what's wrong with you? What's missing? The only thing that was wrong was how you used your mind. So, how you use your mind is completely up to you, as is how you address the things you face. These are there to help you develop; don't cheat yourself by looking for someone else to take care of them. Even if I was somehow able to take care of all the problems facing you, to do so would cause you to lose your potential for growth and salvation. Yet people still bring me these kinds of problems. [Sighs.]

---

17. Avalokitesvara Bodhisattva(觀世音菩薩)**:** The Bodhisattva of Compassion, who hears and responds to the cries of the world, and delivers unenlightened beings from suffering.
Bodhisattva(菩薩)**:** A Bodhisattva is traditionally thought of as an awakened being who remains in this realm in order to continue helping those who are suffering. However, in the most basic sense, a Bodhisattva is the manifestation of our inherent, enlightened essence that is working to save beings, and which uses the non-dual wisdom of enlightenment to help them awaken for themselves.

어떤 때는 울적한 마음에 '에이, 그렇게 하는 거 다 자기 탓인데 어떡해, 할 수 없지. 과거로부터 자기가, 자기 탓으로 온 건데 뭐, 그 복잡한 거를 나한테다가 어찌고저쩌고한다고 그게 해결되나? 자기들이 알아서 해야지.' 이렇게 생각하고는 팽개쳐 버리려고 하다가도 '아니다, 아니다. 그게 아니다.' 이럽니다. 그리고 마음을 다잡습니다.

'나 같은 사람 뭘 보고서 왔겠는가? 나의 이 고깃덩어리를 보고 오지는 않았을 텐데, 나의 마음을 보고 온 것일 텐데, 잘났든 못났든 그 마음이 아리따웁지 못하면 안 되지. 그리고 같이 한마음이 돼 주지 못한다면, 자비가 없어 하나로 끌어안지 못한다면, 그들이 내가 될 수 없고, 그들의 아픔이 내 아픔이 될 수 없고, 내 도량이 될 수 없고, 더불어 같이 살 수 없으니 어찌 그들과 함께 내가 되지 않을 수 있으랴!' 이렇게 마음을 고쳐 잡습니다.

Sometimes, I feel like telling them, "Why do I have to deal with this? This has got nothing to do with me. Why should I have to deal with the results of the things you've done in the past? You made it through your own actions, so take care of it yourself!"

But then I shake this off and remind myself that isn't the right way to think. Those people aren't coming because they think I'm so pretty to look at, they're coming because they're desperate for help.

So, how could I not have compassion for them, how could I not open my heart to them and share their pain? How could I not try to guide them? How could I fulfill my own purpose if I don't have enough compassion to embrace them all as one?

To save just one person may mean hundreds or even thousands of trips to the unseen realm to deal with the causes of the current problems. What finally manifests in the visible realm is the result of vast sweat and toil in this realm of mind. It takes this much hard work to save even a single person.

한 사람을 건지려면 과거로 수백 번, 수천 번 돌아갔다 와야 되고, 이렇게 마음이 이런 짓을 해야만 사람 구하는 것도 가능하게 되는 겁니다. 예를 들어, 과거에 지어 놓은 악업이 많다 보면 그 인연 중에 짐승으로 된 경우도 있고 또 생활 자체도 고통스러워 그쪽으로 관련이 된 몇 집을 걸러서 연관된 문제를 해결해야 될 때도 있습니다.

하지만 여러분들은 알지 못하니까 자기 할 일만 잘하면 돼요. 힘든 일이 생겨도 '과거에 어떠한 사람하고 어떻게 인연이 돼서 이렇게 되었나?' 하고 괴로워할 것도 없습니다. 각자 자기가 할 일을 하면 됩니다.

질문할 분 있으면 질문하세요. 내가 시원찮게 얘기했더라도, 적절한 용어를 잘 몰라서 그런 거니까 여러분들이 지혜롭게 생각해서 잘 들으세요. 그래서 아주 그것을 마음에 꼭 지니고 실천하는 데에 목적을 두시고 진지하게 생각하세요.

For example, when someone has a lot of bad karma, it may be that because of their past actions, some other people have fallen into very bad situations or even been reborn as animals. All of this has to be addressed in order to relieve the first person's suffering. To solve any particular problem, there may be a great many connected issues that also need to be solved.

However, until you've deeply awakened and reached the stage where you can do this, there's no need to worry yourself about what you or others might have done in the past. Just work hard at entrusting the things confronting you right now.

Are there any questions? Even if I haven't made myself clear today, please take your wisdom and good judgment and think about what I've said. Set a goal to apply and put into practice what you've heard today.

질문자 1(여): 스님, 뵙게 돼서 감사합니다. 저는 오늘 한마음선원에 처음 왔습니다. 옆에 있는 이 아이는 고등학교에 갈 제 아들인데요, 항상 주의가 산만하고 불안하고 그렇습니다. 이렇게 마음을 잡지 못하고 방황하고 그러는데 제가 어떻게 하면 좋겠습니까? 좀 가르쳐 주십시오.

큰스님: 학생, 잘 들어 봐. 한마디로 말해서, (왼쪽에 있는 나무를 가리키시며) 저 나무에 뿌리가 있어, 없어?

학생 (남): 있습니다.

큰스님: 있는데, 나무는 흙에 가려서 자기 뿌리를 못 보지?

학생: 예.

큰스님: 사람도 육안으로는 볼 수 없는 자기 영혼의 근본 뿌리가 있어. 그 뿌리를 주인공이라고 이름하는데 그 주인공만이 너의 마음을 모두 이끌어 줄 수가 있어. 네 몸속에 많은 생명들이 있고 많은 의식들이 있기 때문에 그 의식들로 인해서 이 생각 저 생각이 나면서 집중하기가 힘들어지거든.

그러니까 그 의식들을, 그 마음 나오는 거를 다 잡아 줘야 하니까 '주인공, 너만이 나를

Questioner 1 (female): Thank you for this opportunity; this is my first time visiting the Seon Center.

My son [indicating the boy next to her] is about to enter high school, but I'm worried because he often feels uneasy and his attention seems to wander. Is there anything I can do to help this?

Kun Sunim: Young man, please listen carefully. Do you suppose that tree [pointing] has any roots, or not?

Boy: I'm sure it does.

Kun Sunim: Yes, although we can't usually see them because they're covered with dirt, right? Well, each human being also has their own unseen root. We call this root by lots of names, such as foundation, true self, or the true doer, but regardless, it's this root that can guide and take care of you.

Within your body there are many, many living beings, and they also have consciousness. They contribute all kinds of thoughts, which can make it harder for you to concentrate. You have to remember that your foundation is the one in

이끌어 줄 수 있고, 공부 잘하게 할 수 있고, 너의 심부름을 정직하고 진실하고 잘하게 할 수 있잖아.' 하고 네 근본 자리, 주인공에 다 맡겨. 그리고 진짜로 믿어. 네 근본, 네 주인공은 너와 떼려야 뗄 수 없는 네 영원한 친구야. 알았어?

학생: 예.

질문자 2(여): 스님을 이렇게 뵙게 돼서 너무너무 감사합니다. 어떤 복이 있어서 이렇게 스님을 뵙게 됐는지 모르겠습니다. 저는 10년 전에 처음으로 절이라는 데를 갔고 인연 따라서 계속 절을 다녔습니다. 그리고 금년 2월 말에 저와 인연 있는 보살(菩薩)[9]님에게 『한마음요전』[10]을 받았습니다. 『한마음요전』을 보면서 너무나 감사하고, '이런 스님이 지금 현생에 계시구나, 나도 뵐 수 있구나!' 하면서 너무나 기쁘게 생활하고 있습니다.

---

9. 보살(菩薩): 위로는 불법을 닦아 깨달음의 지혜를 얻고, 아래로는 중생을 구제하며 그들이 스스로 깨닫도록 도와주는 부처의 화현. 확대된 의미로 여자 신도를 높여 이르는 말.

10. 한마음요전: 대행큰스님의 가르침을 발췌 및 요약하여 엮은 책. (1993년)

charge and the one that can keep those thoughts from running wild.

So, remind yourself that, "It's you, true nature, my root, that can guide me, and it's you that can help me get through school. You're the one that can let me perceive what's really going on, and respond as needed." And entrust it with whatever situation you find yourself in.

This true nature is your root and your source. It's your eternal and best friend, and is never apart from you.

Questioner 2 (female): I really appreciate this chance to meet you and speak to you directly.

I first visited a Buddhist temple about ten years ago, and attended fairly regularly. Then in February of this year, I was given a copy of your book, *Hanmaum Yojeon* (Essentials of One Mind) by a friend.[18] I found it so inspiring, and was amazed that there are still sunims like you in this day and age. Since then my life has overflowed with gratitude.

---

18. The core of this book has been published in English as *No River to Cross* (Wisdom Publications, 2007).

옛날에는 법은 법대로 저는 저대로 따로따로였는데 지금은 제 생활 속에서 늘 기쁨이 함께합니다.

저의 직장에서도 선원에서 나오는 책들을 다 같이 나누어 보면서 마음을 서로 공유하고 기쁨도 나누는데 그게 아주 큰 즐거움입니다. 그런데 정작 저의 가족들에게는 그게 잘 안 통합니다. 아이들은 다 커서 서울에 있고 저는 대구에 있다 보니까 이 마음법을 전할 길이 없습니다.

아이들이 자랄 때는 제가 그런 걸 너무 몰랐기 때문에, 그런 걸 가르칠 수가 없었고 지금은 상황이 이렇습니다. 제가 어떻게 관해야 이 마음을 전할 수 있을까요? 더군다나 셋째 딸은 이탈리아로 한두 달 후에 가는 모양입니다. 가기 전에 이 마음법을 조금이라도 전해주고 싶습니다. 어떡하면 좋을까요?

큰스님: 좀 전에 내가 말했던 것처럼 나무로 비유해서 설명해 주세요. 그리고 밥 먹을 때 "음식을 먹으니 감사하니?" 하고 물어봐서, 아이가 "감사하다." 하고 대답하면 앞으로는 항상 '음식에 깃든 은혜에, 내 주인공에 감사합니다!' 하고 밥 먹게 하세요.

Before I read that book, I thought Buddhism was something that existed only in Buddhist temples, and wasn't really relevant to my daily life. However, now, the pleasure of the Dharma is always with me in my day-to-day life.

At my job, I've shared your books with my coworkers and several of them have discovered the joy of this spiritual practice. Yet in the case of my own family, I have a hard time sharing it with them. Further, our home is down in Daegu, but my children are going to university in Seoul, so that makes it even harder for me to connect with them.

When they were younger and more willing to listen, I didn't know anything about spiritual practice, and now this is the situation I find myself in. Further, my third daughter is leaving for Italy in a couple of months. Can you give me a method or something so that I can help her understand this Dharma before she leaves?

Kun Sunim: Go ahead and repeat what I just said about a tree and its root. Suggest that before a meal, she simply remind herself of the things she's grateful for, including her family, her root, and so on.

그렇게 간단한 것부터 잘 가르쳐 놓는다면 바로 자기 마음의 보배를 주는 것이므로 재산을 물려주는 것과는 비교할 수도 없죠. 돌에 세워 놔도 살 수 있는 겁니다. 그것이 진짜 재산입니다.

질문자 2: 그런데 스님, 저랑 같이 살고 있지 않거든요. 아이들은 서울에 있습니다.

큰스님: 괜찮아요. 마음으로는 가깝고 멀고가 없어요. 내가 여기 있고 미국에 한 사람이 있다고 합시다. 그런데 마음은 빛보다도 더 빠르기 때문에 찰나에 통할 수 있죠. 이 지구가 한 방으로 돼 있습니다. 한 방! 그러니까 이 한 방에 전구가 여럿이 있다 하더라도 전력은 다 똑같이 들어갈 수 있어요.

질문자 2: 저 혼자라도 가능한가요?

큰스님: 예.

질문자 2: 스님이 말씀해 주신 그 말도 해 주고요?

큰스님: 예, 그럼요.

질문자 2: 네, 스님. 그러겠습니다. 감사합니다.

큰스님: 그렇게 하세요. 자꾸 하다 보면 은연중에 전달이 되고 아이들 마음에도 불이 들어오게끔 돼 있어요. 그리고 책이나 회보, 법문 테이프 같은 걸 좀 보내 주세요. 도움이 될 겁니다.

If you teach her like this, then even though it's very simple, that will grow into a great treasure that will bless her so much more than anything like leaving her a large inheritance. It will become a great treasure that will enable her to take care of whatever kind of difficulties she faces in life.

Questioner 2: But my children aren't living with me; they're in Seoul.

Kun Sunim: It doesn't matter. In mind, there is no distance. Suppose that I'm here and there's someone in the US. We can communicate in an instant, regardless of distance, because mind is faster than even the speed of light. This entire planet is no bigger than a room. A room! No matter how many light bulbs are in a room, the same electricity will illuminate them all instantly.

Questioner 2: And this is possible for me?

Kun Sunim: Yes.

Questioner 2: Okay. I'll be sure to teach my daughter what you've said. Thank you.

Kun Sunim: Good. As you keep working at this, you can connect with her, and quietly communicate with her foundation. In this way,

질문자 3(여): 스님, 지금 말씀하신 분과 상황이 비슷해서 저는 질문 안 하고 지나가려고 했어요. 저한테는 딸은 많고 아들이 하나 있습니다. 그런데 그 애가, 제 마음 같아서는 마음공부[11]를 열심히 좀 했으면 좋겠는데 잘 안 해요.

큰스님: 그거는 부모가 먼저 공부를 해서 능히 이끌어 갈 수 있어야만이 되는 겁니다. 그러니 간단하게 뿌리로 비유하고 나무로 비유해서라도 "너를 끌고 다니는 너를 진짜로 믿어라." 이렇게 해서 생활하면서 체험을 하게 만들어 준다면 그건 안 놓치죠.

질문자 3: 네, 그럴까요? 그런데 제가 선원에서 나온 『마음의 불씨』 같은 책도 읽어 보라고 갖다 주면 그냥 금방 읽고서는 알았다고 그래요. 제가 볼 때는 아닌 것 같아서요.

큰스님: 안다는 것은 '모든 거를 묵묵히, 알지 못한다 해도 아니 되고 안다 해도 아니 되고, 그런 사이에 그냥 묵묵히 이쪽 전깃줄과 저쪽 전깃줄을

---

11. 마음공부: 진정한 자유인이 되기 위해 자신의 마음이 어떻게 작용하고 변하는지를 관찰하고 배우며, 그것을 실제 생활 속에서 응용하고 체험해 보면서 알아 가는 모든 과정을 뜻함.

her own inner light will become brighter. Also, sending some books and tapes from the Seon Center will help, too.

Questioner 3 (female): It seems the question I have is similar to the previous one. In my case, I have several daughters and a son, but my boy doesn't seem interested in learning about this spiritual practice.

Kun Sunim: In cases like that, the parents need to have first developed their own practice to a certain point, then they will be able to guide their children. I think you'd better guide him by telling him the analogy of the tree and its root, and encouraging him to have faith in the true nature that's always leading him. Once he begins to feel and experience this working in his daily life, he won't lose sight of it.

Questioner 3: I gave him a book published by the Center, called *Maum ui Bulsi* (The Living Spark Within) and although he read it and said he understood it, it didn't seem so to me.

Kun Sunim: Listen, if you want him to know about this, then stop trying to do it through words.

맞대서 불이 들어올 수 있게끔 해 놓으면 자연스럽게 통하게 돼서 흐르는 그런 것'이 진짜 아는 거예요.

그러니까 진짜 알게 해줄 수 있는 방법은 당신 주인공에다 '저 애도 자기 주인공의 밝은 등불을 찾게끔 바로 당신만이 할 수 있어.' 하고 맡기는 것뿐이에요. 그 마음이 진정으로 통하게 되면 벌써 그 아이 마음속에 등불이 켜지게끔 돼 있습니다.

질문자 3: 네, 대단히 감사합니다.

질문자 4(여): 저는 금왕지원 학생회에 다니는 고3 학생입니다. 이렇게 큰스님을 뵙게 되어서 너무너무 좋아요. 여기 질문하러 오기 전까지는 되게 헷갈리는 게 많았었는데 큰스님 뵙고 나서 바로 정말 많은 부분이 정리가 됐어요. 여러 스님들께서 "세상을 다 준다고 해도 바꿀 수 없는 그런 묘법을 만났으니까 모든 걸 다 걸어야 한다." 하는 말씀을 많이 해주셨는데 제가 혼돈스러웠어요. 그런데 큰스님을 뵙는 순간 '그냥 정말 나는 모든 걸 다 걸고 죽을 때까지 이 길을 걸어야 되겠다.'라는 그런 생각이 들었어요.

Let go of any idea that you know something, or even that you don't know something, and just let the electrical wire that is your mind make contact with the wire that is your son's side. When they connect, energy and light will flow naturally between both sides. This is how to help him know the essence of spiritual practice.

Anyway, it would be better for you to entrust the following, "This true nature, Juingong, will help him find the bright light within himself." If you truly let go and entrust this, then that will be communicated and he'll start to see his own light.

Questioner 3: I understand. Thank you so much for this.

Questioner 4 (female): Hello. I'm a high school senior. Before I saw you today there were a lot of confusing things in my life that I wanted to ask you about. However, as I sat down here today, all of those disappeared, and the only thought that arose within me was that I will walk this path of attaining the Dharma until the end of my life. I can only agree with those sunims who said that this treasure is worth more than anything else in the world.

요즘에는 생각을 하려고 해도 생각이 깊게 잘 안되고, 제 안을 들여다 보면 뭔가가 막 이렇게 떠다니는 것 같아요. 생겨났다 없어졌다 하는 것도 많고, 또 그냥 그거를 보게 되기도 하고요. 그게 뭔지는 잘 모르겠는데 뭐랄까, 까마득하다 하는 그런 느낌도 들고, 한순간 가슴이 너무 답답해져 오는 거를 느끼고 그러거든요.

물론 계속 주인공에 관하면서 이렇게 공부해 가지만 큰스님께 가르침 받고 싶어서 나왔습니다.

큰스님: 지금 걸음마도 걷지 못하는 아기가 젖병 하나 들고 잘 먹고 크면 되지 뭐 그렇게 생각이 많아? 똥 누면 똥 치워 주겠다, 좋은 잠자리가 있으니 졸리면 그냥 잠자고 그러면 되지, 안 그래? 허허허.

무조건 믿어. 저 나무들이 무조건 자기 뿌리를 믿고 살고 있어. "너, 네 뿌리를 진짜로 믿고 사니?" 하고 저 나무들한테 가서 물어봐. 그렇게 "진짜로 믿고 사니?" 하고 묻는다면 묻는 자가 어리석어. 그렇지? 뿌리가 이미 있으니 거기에 달려 있는 것들에는 벌써 싹이 나서 살고 있는데 "너, 뿌리를 진짜 믿니?" 이러면 얼마나 우스운 얘기야, 안 그래?

Lately, I've been feeling very emotional and unstable, and this has made it hard for me to concentrate on anything. When I observe my thoughts, it seems like all kinds of strange things are popping into my mind, flying around within me, and then disappearing, only to be immediately replaced by new ones. I can't quite describe this right; but it fills me with an irrational fear sometimes, and makes me feel suffocated.

Of course, I'm working at entrusting all of this to Juingong, but I was wondering if you had any advice for me.

Kun Sunim: Imagine that you're an infant who can't even walk yet. The only thing a baby needs to do is hold onto the nipple and keep suckling. What is the point of an infant worrying about anything? If it takes a poo, it will be cleaned up. If she needs to sleep, a bed will be provided. The only thing a baby needs to do is feed when she's hungry and sleep when she feels tired. What else is there to worry about?

The only thing you need to do is believe in your root. Completely rely upon it. All those

너도 너를 형성시킨 근본이 있으니 이 세상에 이렇게 태어나 살고 있는 거고 그렇기 때문에, 상대가 있고 세상이 있는 거야. 그러니까 너를 형성시킨 너부터 믿어야 될 거 아니야? 그냥 간단하게 너를 있게 한 영원한 자기의 생명, 주인공을 진짜로 믿어 봐!

그걸 여러 가지로 이름을 부르는데 이름은 중요하지 않아. 이름이 좋든 그르든 말이야. 어찌 됐던 '주인공!' 하면 둘이 아닌 이 한 개체가, 나와 내 근본이 둘이 아닌 내가 살고 있는 걸 말하는 거야. 그런데 이게 고정된 게 없이 살고 있거든.

질문자 4: 지난번에 수련회를 다녀왔는데, 거기서 공부를 참 많이 했어요. 프로그램 중에 밤에 산행을 하는 게 있었는데 담력 테스트 비슷한 그런 거였어요.

그런데 저희 조가 길을 잘못 들어서 오랫동안 산을 헤매다가 새벽 2시 정도에 산에서 내려왔어요.

trees [pointing outside] live by relying upon their root. To ask them if they believe in their root is like asking a person if they have a head. Absurd. When you see the leaves and branches, in that instant you automatically know that tree has a root.

You, too, have a root, a foundation that formed you. It's because of this that you were born with this body and are able to perceive everything you encounter and everything in front of you. So, instead of chasing after those things, doesn't it make more sense to rely upon the root that is the source of all that? You are the manifestation of this. Believe in the essence that's formed you, the eternal essence that's the source of your life!

People call it by all kinds of names, but just know that because you're living here now, your Juingong is also here, working together with all the lives in your body, continuously flowing and changing.

Questioner 4: I just attended the summer youth retreat, and experienced something very interesting. There was a mountain hiking

그때 비도 많이 오고 산에서 오랫동안 헤매다 보니 잠깐 꿈꾼 것 같은 그런 느낌이 있었지만 그래도 무섭다는 생각은 하나도 없었어요. 단지, 정말 믿을 거라고는 주인공밖에 없다는 생각을 했었어요.

큰스님: 잘했어. 정말 그렇게만 자꾸 해 나가면 일등 될 거야. 하하하….

질문자 4: 그때, 정말 큰스님도 계속 찾고, 주인공도 막 찾고 하면서 내려왔는데 그 모든 게 너무너무 고마웠어요. 정말 완벽하게, 나를 공부시키려고 모든 게 그렇게 돌아간 것 같았어요.

program, which was more like a courage test, where we would walk down a trail in the dark as a team.

However my team got lost about halfway down, and strayed quite far into the forest. We'd started at 9 p.m., but it was about 2 a.m. before we finally found our way back to the Seon Center. It even rained quite hard while we were lost.

The whole time, it was clear to me that the only thing I could believe in was Juingong, and I wasn't scared a bit, even though the situation could have turned out quite bad. As I think back on it, the experience feels like a dream.

Kun Sunim: You handled that very well. If you keep going forward like that, you'll be outstanding in whatever you do.

Questioner 4: When we were lost I kept myself focused on Juingong and what you've taught. Even though we were lost and wet, I felt such deep appreciation as we made our way, and now I think that everything that happened was to help me realize how this fundamental mind works.

큰스님: 우리는 인간으로 태어났으면 진리를 참구하고 공부하고 가야 되는 거거든. 그런데 자기가 공부한다는 생각을 못 하고 자꾸 배우러 어디로 쫓아다니고, 붙들려고 하고, 잡으려고 하고, 그러고 돌아다녀. 그런데 자기 자신부터 알아야 된다는 얘기야. 믿어야 되고 알아야 하고.

그러니까 그렇게 제대로 공부하려고 애를 쓸 때면 빈손, 즉 말하자면 보이지 않는 손들이 다 가서 이렇게 붙들어 줘. 그 나무들이 전부 관세음보살(觀世音菩薩)[12]이 되고, 그 나무들이 전부 보살들이 돼. 길잡이가 되고.

질문자 4: 큰스님께 너무너무 감사드립니다. 앞으로도 열심히 하겠습니다.

큰스님: 그래. 이 묘한 도리를 말로 어떻게 다 할 수 있겠니. 자기가 스스로 하면서 터득해 나가야지.

---

12. 관세음보살(觀世音菩薩): 세간의 괴로움으로부터 구원을 원하는 소리를 듣고 이에 응하여 고통으로부터 중생을 대자대비한 마음으로 구제하는 보살. 산스크리트로는 아바로키테슈바라(Avalokitesvara)인데, 이는 곧 자재롭게 보는 이[觀自在], 자재로운 관찰이란 뜻으로서, 세상의 모든 것을 자재롭게 관조하여 보살핀다는 뜻.

Kun Sunim: If you've managed to evolve all the way up to a human being, then you have to take advantage of that, and work hard to deepen your spiritual level and seek to realize the truth.

Why? Because only humans, among all the animals, have the unique ability for growth and self-reflection. Many people don't realize that everything in life is an opportunity to practice, so they run around here and there looking for something fascinating, or trying to find some fixed concept they can cling onto.

But the real point of your life is to know who you are. This is what you have to know. When you have faith in your essence, this faith will lead you to who you truly are. When you work at this, when you make an effort towards this, then unseen hands will help and protect you. Even the trees around you will turn into merciful Bodhisattvas that will guide you.

Questioner 4: Thank you so much for this wonderful teaching! I will work hard to realize all this for myself.

Kun Sunim: Good! Words are so inadequate at describing workings of our fundamental

질문자 5(남): 저는 대학원에 다니는 학생인데요, 학교 일정이 있어서 시간이 바쁠 때는 법회에 참석하지 못하는 경우가 있었습니다.

지난 몇 달 동안 바쁘다는 핑계로 법회에 안 왔었는데, 그러다 보니 생활이 좀 무기력해진 것 같고, 일이 좀 잘 안되는 것 같아서 다시 법회에 나오고 있습니다. 몸은 좀 힘들더라도 그렇게 하니 생활하는데 자신감이 더 생기는 것 같습니다.

그런데 큰스님께서는 불교를 기복 신앙으로 하지 말라고 하셨는데 저의 경우는 법회에 참석하면 뭔지 일이 잘 풀리는 것 같은 그런 기분이에요. 그래서 시간이 별로 없어도 와야만 할 것 같은 그런 생각이 있거든요. 피곤해서 가끔은 졸더라도요. 그런데 이거 자체가 하나의 기복 신앙이 되는 게 아닌가 하는 그런 생각이 듭니다.

mind. It's just so incredible! Now, work hard and experience this for yourself.

Questioner 5 (male): I'm a graduate student, and when my schedule is too busy, I sometimes skip the monthly Dharma talks here, telling myself that I'm too busy or tired. However, after doing this for several months, I began to feel listless, and things in my life weren't turning out well.

So, I started attending the Dharma talks again, even though I was still tired, and I began to feel more connected and positive about everything around me.

My question is this: You've taught us not to rely upon outer things, nor to get caught up in praying to outside powers, and to instead rely upon only our true self. But in my case, I feel like my life goes better when I attend the monthly Dharma talks. If I come to the Dharma talk everything works out better than when I skip the monthly Dharma talks. But lately I've started to worry that all this is just another form of chasing after blessings or good luck.

큰스님: 하하하…. 아니, 그러면 사는 게 전부 기복이죠. 가고 싶은 데 가는 것이 왜 기복입니까? 그건 당당한 바로 자기 자성의 발현이죠. 대상을 놓고서 빌고 타의에서 찾지 말라 하는 거지 자기 자성에서 저절로 일어나는 건 어떤 거든지 그냥 자성 그대로 법이죠.

질문자 6(남): 질문을 안 하려고 했는데, 이 문제는 다른 법우님들도 조금 궁금해하시는 것 같아서 그냥 질문드리겠습니다. 부모가 자식에 끄달리다 보니 부모와 자식 간의 뜻이 안 맞아서 서로 어긋나는 일이 많거든요. 그래서 부모님은 부모님대로 힘들고 자식은 자식대로 힘듭니다. 이러한 부모와 자식 간의 관계를 영원히 벗어나는 '딱' 소리 나는 가르침을 부탁드립니다.

큰스님: '딱' 소리가 나게 벗어나고 싶으면 자기가 '딱' 소리 나게 하면 되죠.

아니, 지금 당신이 배가 고파 죽겠는데 대신 내가 밥을 먹는다고 한다면 당신이 배가 부르겠습니까?

질문자 6: 아뇨. 부르지 않습니다.

Kun Sunim: [laughs] How could wanting to go somewhere the Dharma is being taught be begging for something outside yourself? Instead, it is your true essence very straightforwardly revealing itself. What I had meant was to not set up some outer object or power and then pray to it.

Questioner 6 (male): I'd like to ask about something that I think applies to many people. A lot of parents tend to meddle in or try to control their children's lives. Kids often resent this, and their relationship becomes more and more strained and uncomfortable for both the parents and the kids. Is there some method that can completely sweep away these kinds of problems?

Kun Sunim: If you want to completely change your relationships, then you have to completely entrust them. You're the one who has to do it. Will you become full if I eat your breakfast? No.

Our lives are a ceaseless unfolding, a ceaseless flowing and responding. When we're hungry, we go and eat. When there's pressure in our bowels, we find a toilet. And when our body is exhausted, we take a break.

큰스님: 당연히 아니죠? 배고프면 먹고, 먹었으니 똥 마려우면 누고, 졸리면 자고 할 수 있는, 그대로 여여(如如)[13]하게 사는 것이 우리 인생이라 할 수 있습니다.

예를 들어, 종을 하나 치더라도 바람과도 인연이 맞아야 되고, 종 치는 사람과도 인연이 맞아야 되고, 또 그걸 듣는 사람과도 맞아야 그 소리가 제대로 잘 쳐진 거겠죠.

자식과 부모의 인연이란 것도 육(肉)의 인연에 따라 끼리끼리 만나는 겁니다. 육이라 했다고 겉모습을 이야기하는 게 아니에요.

이 세상을 보세요. 금은 금대로 모여 있고 넝마는 넝마대로 모이지 않습니까? 중은 중들대로 끼리끼리 모여 있고, 속인은 속인대로 모여 있고, 정치인은 정치인들대로 모여 있고, 애들은 애들대로 모여서 놀고 그래요. 상점에 가 보세요. 사과는 사과대로 놓여 있고 배는 배대로 놓여 있습니다. 받는 사람이 깡통이면 주는 사람도 깡통이겠죠.

---

13. 여여(如如): 만물만생이 평등하고 차별 없이, 어디에도 머물지 않고 끊임없이 흘러 돌아가고 있는 그대로의 모습. 일체가 고정됨이 없이 돌아가는 진실의 모습을 말하며, 이러한 진리의 흐름에 부합하는 삶을 살아가는 것을 여여한 삶이라 함.

If you strike that bell over there [pointing], it will produce a sound according to your skill at striking it. Those people who decided to come here today will then hear it, and, according to their preferences, will think that it's a good sound or not.

The interactions between parents and children are the same. Your similar karma and levels of spirituality drew you together, and leads to all different kinds of interactions.

You see this with everything in the world. Gold is put together with gold, and iron is gathered together with iron, isn't it? Monks gather with other monks, lay people gather with lay people, politicians spend time with other politicians, and children go and play with other children. Even in grocery stores you see this: apples are placed with apples, and pears with pears.

So, whatever is happening in your own family right now is the result of your own karma and spirituality; it's drawn you together, and it shapes how you respond to each other. If you want to change how things are now, then you

그러니까 똑같이 끼리끼리 모였기 때문에 생기는 일입니다. 그러니 업보에 대한 문제를 그 업보가 나오는 데다가 되놔라 이런 소립니다.

내가 항상 말하죠? 자식이 그저 공부 안 한다, 뭐 잘못한다, 나가서 자고 안 들어온다 별일을 다 한다 하더라도 부모 입장에서 화만 내지 말고 아주 부드럽게 말해 주라고요.

부드러운 말과 행동으로 "애, 너 나가서 배는 안 곯았니? 어디서 잤니?" 아주 이렇게 부드럽게 말이에요. "네 일생을 생각할 땐 네가 알아서 해야 되지 않겠어?" 하고 자식 입장에서 부드럽게 해 줘야 자식의 마음이 따뜻한 데로 고이게 되지 않겠어요?

have to dissolve the causes that are shaping your circumstances. This is why I keep telling you to entrust all those problems back to your foundation, because that's where they've arisen from, and that's the place that can dissolve them.

I've said this before, but even if your kids ignore their studies, even if they stay out all night, even if they get picked up by the police, don't just yell at them. Don't speak down to them.

Instead, speak with a kind voice. Ask if they've eaten. Ask if they got any sleep. Be tender and kind. If you give advice, do it from the perspective of their well being, "You're the one who's in charge of your life, and the one who needs to take care of it. Please think about your future from time to time."

If you want to be able to help them, your speech has to be gentle – from their viewpoint! If they see your heart as warm and kind, how could they not want to spend more time in such a home. Through mind, you need to create a warm and friendly environment.

When you entrust all of these kinds of problems to your foundation, they become smaller

마음을 잡아야지 몸뚱이를 잡아서 되는 게 아니에요. 그렇게 모든 문제들을 차츰차츰 내 근본 자리에 되맡기면서 가다 보면 문제들이 사그라들고 해결이 됩니다.

전등과 스위치가 이미 연결되어 있어서 스위치를 올리면 불이 들어오듯이, 부모 자식 간도 마찬가지입니다. 부모와 자식 간이란 것은 근본에서 서로 알기 때문에 이미 자동적으로 가설이 돼 있어요. 이미 가설이 된 거니까 내 주인공에다가 내가 모든 거를 맡기고 부드럽게 얘기하고 그러면 상대방의 마음속에도 불이 들어오게 돼 있거든요. 그러니까 둘이 아니라는 뜻이에요.

원수처럼 지내던 모자가 있었는데 둘이 매일 싸우면서 고통스럽게 지내다가 어느 날 한순간 그렇게 망나니처럼 굴던 아이가 "어머니, 독 닦아 드릴까요? 뭐해 드릴까요?" 그러더랍니다. 마음이 둘이 아니기 때문에 그동안의 마음이 통해 서로 연결이 된 겁니다.

and smaller, and eventually disappear. Parents and children are all connected by this foundation, and when you practice like this, it's like turning on the electricity to a room: in that instant, all the light bulbs in the room become brighter. Parents and children are living in the same room like this.

Because you both already know that you are family, this unseen connection works even stronger. When you entrust your concerns there and speak gently to your child, that entrusting and intention is instantly communicated to your child's fundamental mind. As soon as your light comes on, theirs also becomes bright.

There was a mother and son who had terrible quarrels. They fought all the time and went at each other as if they were enemies. But the mother began to learn this practice of entrusting, and kept at it. One day, her son came home just as she was having a hard time washing the big kimchi pots in their yard. Without his mom saying a word, he just pitched in and helped her move and clean them.

That was the first sign of a transformation that eventually made him seem like a completely

자기 주인공에다 모든 걸 그냥 놓으면 상대방한테도 불이 들어오게 돼 있어요. 가설이 돼 있거든요.

그러니 상대방 탓만 하지 말고 지혜로운 마음을 내세요. 그런 마음이라야만이 융통성 있게 집안을 이끌어 나갈 수 있습니다.

different person. It was the result of the communication between them that was occurring because his mother was working at letting go. As her mind became brighter, his did, too.

Because you are inherently connected with others, as you entrust your problems to your essence – your foundation – the light that arises from that entrusting also grows brighter within the other person. So there's no reason to blame others; instead, work on using your mind wisely.

If you can go forward with this kind of wisdom, how could your family not be happy and successful?

한마음출판사의 마음을 밝혀 주는 도서

- A Thousand Hands of Compassion
  만가지 꽃이 피고 만가지 열매 익어
  : 대행큰스님의 뜻으로 푼 천수경 (한글/영어)
  [2010 iF Communication Design Award 수상]
- Wake Up And Laugh (영어)
- No River To Cross, No Raft To Find (영어)
- It's Hard To Say (영어) (절판)
- My Heart Is A Golden Buddha (영어)
- Touching The Earth (영어)
- 생활 속의 참선수행 (시리즈) (한글/영어)
  1. 죽어야 나를 보리라
     (To Discover Your True Self, "I" Must Die)
  2. 함이 없이 하는 도리
     (Walking Without A Trace)
  3. 맡겨놓고 지켜봐라
     (Let Go And Observe)
  4. 마음은 보이지 않는 행복의 창고
     (Mind, Treasure House Of Happiness)
  5. 일체를 용광로에 넣어라
     (The Furnace Within Yourself)
  6. 온 우주를 살리는 마음의 불씨
     (The Spark That Can Save The Universe)
  7. 한마음의 위력
     (The Infinite Power Of One Mind)
  8. 일체를 움직이는 그 자리
     (In The Heart Of A Moment)

9. 한마음 한뜻이 되어
   (One With The Universe)
10. 지구보존
    (Protecting The Earth)
11. 진짜 통하게 되면
    (Inherent Connections)
12. 잘 돼야 돼!
    (Finding A Way Forward)
13. 믿는 만큼 行한 만큼
    (Faith In Action, 2017 new)

- 내 마음은 금부처 (한글)
- 건널 강이 어디 있으랴 (한글)
- 처음 시작하는 마음공부1 (한글)
- El Camino Interior (스페인어)
- Vida De La Maestra Seon Daehaeng (스페인어)
- Enseñanzas De La Maestra Daehaeng (스페인어)
- Práctica Del Seon En La Vida Diaria (Colección) (스페인어/영어)
    1. Una Semilla Inherente Alimenta El Universo
       (The Spark That Can Save The Universe)
- Si Te Lo Propones, No Hay Imposibles (스페인어)
- 人生不是苦海 (번체자 중국어) (개정판)
- 无河可渡 (간체자 중국어)
- 我心是金佛 (간체자 중국어) (개정판)

해외출판사에서 출판된 한마음도서

- Wake Up And Laugh
  Wisdom Publications, 미국

- No River To Cross
  (*No River To Cross, No Raft To Find* 영어판)
  Wisdom Publications, 미국

- Wie Fließendes Wasser
  (*My Heart Is A Golden Buddha* 독일어판)
  Goldmann Arkana-Random House, 독일

- Ningún Río Que Cruzar
  (*No River To Cross* 스페인어판)
  Kailas Editorial, S.L., 스페인

- Umarmt Von Mitgefühl
  ('만가지 꽃이 피고 만가지 열매 익어':
  대행큰스님의 뜻으로 푼 천수경 독일어판)
  Diederichs-Random House, 독일

- 我心是金佛
  (*My Heart Is A Golden Buddha* 번체자 중국어판)
  橡樹林文化出版, 대만

- Vertraue Und Lass Alles Los
  (*No River To Cross* 독일어판)
  Goldmann Arkana-Random House, 독일

- Wache Auf Und Lache
  (*Wake Up And Laugh* 독일어판)
  Theseus, 독일

- Дзэн И Просветление
  (No River To Cross 러시아어판)
  Amrita-Rus, 러시아

- Sup Cacing Tanah
  (*My Heart Is A Golden Buddha* 인도네시아어판)
  PT Gramedia, 인도네시아

- Không có sông nào để vượt qua
  (*No River To Cross* 베트남어판)
  Vien Chieu, 베트남

Books by Daehaeng Kun Sunim
-available through Hanmaum Publications

- Touching The Earth (English)
- A Thousand Hands of Compassion (bilingual, Korean/English) [received **2010 iF communication design Award**]
- Wake Up And Laugh (English)
- No River To Cross, No Raft To Find (English)
- My Heart Is A Golden Buddha (English)
- One Mind: Principles (English)
- *Practice in Daily Life* (Series) (bilingual, Korean/English)
    1. To Discover Your True Self, "I" Must Die
    2. Walking Without A Trace
    3. Let Go And Observe
    4. Mind, Treasure House Of Happiness
    5. The Furnace Within Yourself
    6. The Spark That Can Save The Universe
    7. The Infinite Power Of One Mind
    8. In The Heart Of A Moment
    9. One With The Universe
    10. Protecting The Earth
    11. Inherent Connections
    12. Finding A Way Forward
    13. Faith In Action (2017 new)
- *건널 강이 어디 있으랴* (Korean)
- *내 마음은 금부처* (Korean)
- El Camino Interior (Spanish)
- Vida De La Maestra Seon Daehaeng (Spanish)

- Enseñanzas De La Maestra Daehaeng (Spanish)
- Práctica Del Seon En La Vida Diaria (Series) (bilingual, Spanish/English)
    1. Una Semilla Inherente Alimenta El Universo
- Si Te Lo Propones, No Hay Imposibles (Spanish)
- 人生不是苦海 (Traditional Chinese) (new edition)
- 无河可渡 (Simplified Chinese)
- 我心是金佛 (Simplified Chinese) (new edition)

-Books available through other Publishers

- No River To Cross
  Wisdom Publications, U.S.A.

- Wake Up And Laugh
  Wisdom Publications, U.S.A.

- Wie Fließendes Wasser
  German edition of *My Heart Is A Golden Buddha*
  Goldmann Arkana-Random House, Germany

- Vertraue Und Lass Alles Los
  German edition of *No River To Cross*
  Goldmann Arkana-Random House, Germany

- Umarmt Von Mitgefühl
  German edition of *A Thousand Hands Of Compassion*
  Diederichs-Random House, Germany

- Wache Auf Und Lache
  German edition of *Wake Up And Laugh*
  Theseus, Germany

- Ningún Río Que Cruzar
  Spanish edition of *No River To Cross*
  Kailas Editorial, S.L., Spain

- 我心是金佛
  Traditional Chinese edition of *My Heart Is A Golden Buddha*
  Oak Tree Publishing Co., Taiwan

- Дзэн И Просветление
  Russian edition of *No River To Cross*
  Amrita-Rus, Russia

- Sup Cacing Tanah
  Indonesian edition of *My Heart Is A Golden Buddha*
  PT Gramedia, Indonesia
- Không có sông nào để vượt qua
  Vietnam edition of *No River To Cross*
  Vien Chieu, Vietnam

한마음선원본원

경기도 안양시 만안구 경수대로 1282 (석수동, 한마음선원)
(우) 13908
Tel : 82-31-470-3100   Fax : 82-31-470-3116
홈페이지 : http://www.hanmaum.org
이메일 : jongmuso@hanmaum.org

국내지원

강릉지원   (우)25565 강원도 강릉시 하평5길 29 (포남동)
            TEL:(033) 651-3003   FAX:(033) 652-0281

공주지원   (우)32522 충청남도 공주시 사곡면 위안양골길 157-61
            TEL:(041) 852-9100   FAX:(041) 852-9105

광명선원   (우)27638 충청북도 음성군 금왕읍 대금로 1402
            TEL:(043) 877-5000   FAX:(043) 877-2900

광주지원   (우)61965 광주광역시 서구 운천로 204번길 23-1 (치평동)
            TEL:(062) 373-8801   FAX:(062) 373-0174

대구지원   (우)42152 대구광역시 수성구 수성로 41길 76(중동)
            TEL:(053) 767-3100   FAX:(053) 765-1600

목포지원   (우)58696 전라남도 목포시 백년대로 266번길 31-1 (상동)
            TEL:(061) 284-1771   FAX:(061) 284-1770

문경지원   (우)36937 경상북도 문경시 산양면 봉서1길 10
            TEL:(054) 555-8871   FAX:(054) 556-1989

부산지원   (우)49113 부산광역시 영도구 함지로 79번길 23-26 (동삼동)
            TEL:(051) 403-7077   FAX:(051) 403-1077

울산지원   (우)44200 울산광역시 북구 달래골길 26-12 (천곡동)
            TEL:(052) 295-2335   FAX:(052) 295-2336

제주지원 (우)63308 제주특별자치도 제주시 황사평6길 176-1 (영평동)
TEL:(064) 727-3100   FAX:(064) 727-0302

중부경남 (우)50871 경상남도 김해시 진영읍 하계로35
TEL:(055) 345-9900   FAX:(055) 346-2179

진주지원 (우)52602 경상남도 진주시 미천면 오방로 528-40
TEL:(055) 746-8163   FAX:(055) 746-7825

청주지원 (우)28540 충청북도 청주시 청원구 교서로 109
TEL:(043) 259-5599   FAX:(043) 255-5599

통영지원 (우)53021 경상남도 통영시 광도면 조암길 45-230
TEL:(055) 643-0643   FAX:(055) 643-0642

포항지원 (우)37635 경상북도 포항시 북구 우창로 59 (우현동)
TEL:(054) 232-3163   FAX:(054) 241-3503

Anyang Headquarters of Hanmaum Seonwon

1282 Gyeongsu-daero, Manan-gu, Anyang-si,
Gyeonggi-do, 13908, Republic of Korea
Tel: (82-31) 470-3175 / Fax: (82-31) 470-3209
www.hanmaum.org/eng
onemind@hanmaum.org

Overseas Branches of Hanmaum Seonwon

ARGENTINA
Buenos Aires
Miró 1575, CABA, C1406CVE, Rep. Argentina
Tel: (54-11) 4921-9286 / Fax: (54-11) 4921-9286
http://hanmaumbsas.org

Tucumán
Av. Aconquija 5250, El Corte, Yerba Buena,
Tucumán, T4107CHN, Rep. Argentina
Tel: (54-381) 425-1400
www.hanmaumtuc.org

BRASIL
São Paulo
R. Newton Prado 540, Bom Retiro
Sao Paulo, CEP 01127-000, Brasil
Tel: (55-11) 3337-5291
www.hanmaumbr.org

CANADA
Toronto
20 Mobile Dr., North York, Ontario M4A 1H9, Canada
Tel: (1-416) 750-7943
www.hanmaum.org/toronto

GERMANY
Kaarst
Broicherdorf Str. 102, 41564 Kaarst, Germany
Tel: (49-2131) 969551 / Fax: (49-2131) 969552
www.hanmaum-zen.de

THAILAND
Bangkok
86/1 Soi 4 Ekamai Sukhumvit 63
Bangkok, Thailand
Tel: (66-2) 391-0091
www.hanmaum.org/cafe/thaihanmaum

USA
Chicago
7852 N. Lincoln Ave., Skokie, IL 60077, USA
Tel: (1-847) 674-0811
www.hanmaum.org/chicago

Los Angeles
1905 S. Victoria Ave., L.A., CA 90016, USA
Tel: (1-323) 766-1316
www.hanmaum.org/la

New York
144-39, 32 Ave., Flushing, NY 11354, USA
Tel: (1-718) 460-2019 / Fax: (1-718) 939-3974
www.juingong.org

Washington D.C.
7807 Trammel Rd., Annandale, VA 22003, USA
Tel: (1-703) 560-5166
www.hanmaum.org/wa

책에 관한 문의나 주문을 하실 분들은
아래의 연락처로 문의해 주십시오.

한마음국제문화원/한마음출판사
경기도 안양시 만안구 경수대로 1282 (우)13908
전화: (82-31) 470-3175
팩스: (82-31) 470-3209
e-mail: onemind@hanmaum.org
www.hanmaumbooks.org

If you would like more information about these books or
would like to order copies of them,
please call or write to:

Hanmaum International Culture Institute
Hanmaum Publications
1282 Gyeongsu-daero, Manan-gu, Anyang-si,
Gyeonggi-do, 13908,
Republic of Korea
Tel: (82-31) 470-3175
Fax: (82-31) 470-3209
e-mail: onemind@hanmaum.org
www.hanmaumbooks.org